A-Z DART[...]

C000143505

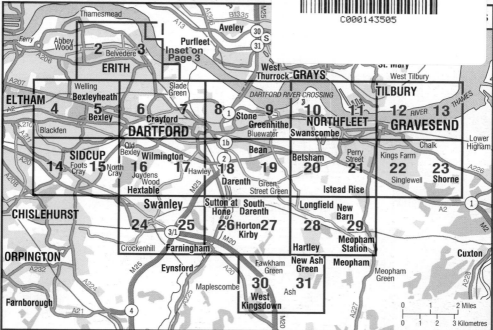

Map index showing areas including: Thamesmead, Aveley, Ferry, Abbey Wood, Belvedere, Purfleet Inset on Page 3, West Thurrock, GRAYS, St. Mary, West Tilbury, ERITH, Welling, Bexleyheath, Slade Green, DARTFORD RIVER CROSSING, TILBURY, ELTHAM, Bexley, Crayford, DARTFORD, Stone, Greenhithe, NORTHFLEET, RIVER, GRAVESEND, THAMES, Blackfen, Bluewater, Swanscombe, Lower Higham, SIDCUP, Old Bexley, Wilmington, Hawley, Bean, Betsham, Perry Street, Kings Farm, Chalk, Foots Cray, North Cray, Joydens Wood, Darenth, Green Street Green, Singlewell, Shorne, Hextable, Istead Rise, CHISLEHURST, Swanley, Sutton at Hone, South Darenth, Horton Kirby, Longfield, New Barn, Meopham Station, Cuxton, ORPINGTON, Crockenhill, Farningham, Hartley, Meopham, Meopham Green, Farnborough, Eynsford, Maplescombe, Fawkham Green, New Ash Green, Ash, West Kingsdown

Reference

Motorway M25	**Railway** Station, Level Crossing, Tunnel	**Police Station** ▲
A Road A226		**Post Office** ★
B Road B262	**Built-Up Area** BOND ST.	**Toilet with Facilities for the Disabled** ♿
Dual Carriageway	**Local Authority Boundary**	**Educational Establishment**
One-Way Street Traffic flow on A roads is indicated by a heavy line on the drivers' left. →	**Postcode Boundary**	**Hospital or Hospice**
Restricted Access	**Map Continuation** 16	**Industrial Building**
Pedestrianized Road	**Church or Chapel** †	**Leisure or Recreational Facility**
Track & Footpath	**Fire Station** ■	**Place of Interest**
Residential Walkway	**Hospital** Ⓗ	**Public Building**
Junction Name DARTFORD HEATH	**House Numbers** A & B Roads only	**Shopping Centre or Market**
	Information Centre 🅸	**Other Selected Buildings**
	National Grid Reference 550	

Scale 1:19,000
3⅓ inches (8.47 cm) to 1 mile
5.26 cm to 1 kilometre

0 ¼ ½ ¾ Mile
0 250 500 750 Metres 1 Kilometre

Copyright of Geographers' A-Z Map Company Limited

Head Office:
Fairfield Road, Borough Green, Sevenoaks, Kent TN15 8PP
Telephone 01732 781000 (General Enquiries & Trade Sales)
Showrooms:
44 Gray's Inn Road, London WC1X 8HX
Telephone 020 7440 9500 (Retail Sales)
www.a-zmaps.co.uk

Ordnance Survey® This product includes mapping data licensed from Ordnance Survey® with the permission of the Controller of Her Majesty's Stationery Office.
© Crown Copyright 2001. Licence number 100017302
Copyright © Geographers' A-Z Map Co. Ltd. 2001
Edition 3 2001   Edition 3A 2002 (Part Revision)

F G H J K **13**

68 69 77

Bowaters Farm

Mariner Cotts.
PRINCESS GORDON RD
MARGARET RD
Castle Farm
Church Green

1

Coalhouse Fort & Thameside Aviation Museum

East Tilbury Marshes

2

Valve Compound

Water Tower

76

Coalhouse Point

Jetty

3

Wharf

T H A M E S

4

EACH

THURROCK
GRAVESHAM

175

Causeway

5

Shornmead Fort

Saxon Shore Way

Pav.

SHORNE MARSHES

6

Milton Rifle Range

74

EASTCOURT

MARSHES

es & Medway Canal (disused)

DA12

7

Great Clane Lane Marshes

FILBOROUGH MARSHES

Fish Pond

Queen's Farm

QUEENS FARM ROAD

F G H **23** J K

68 69

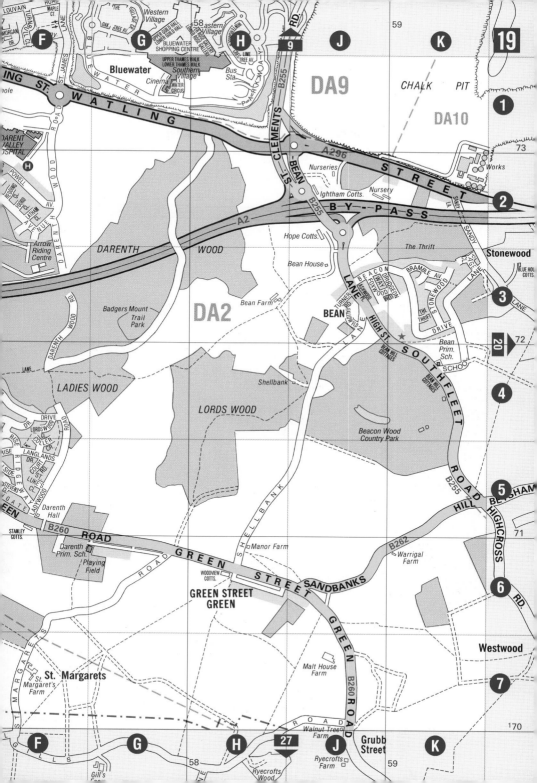

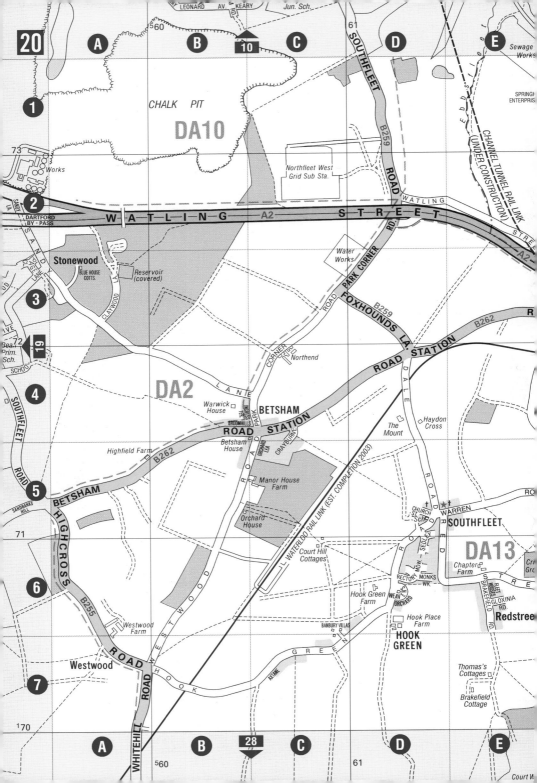

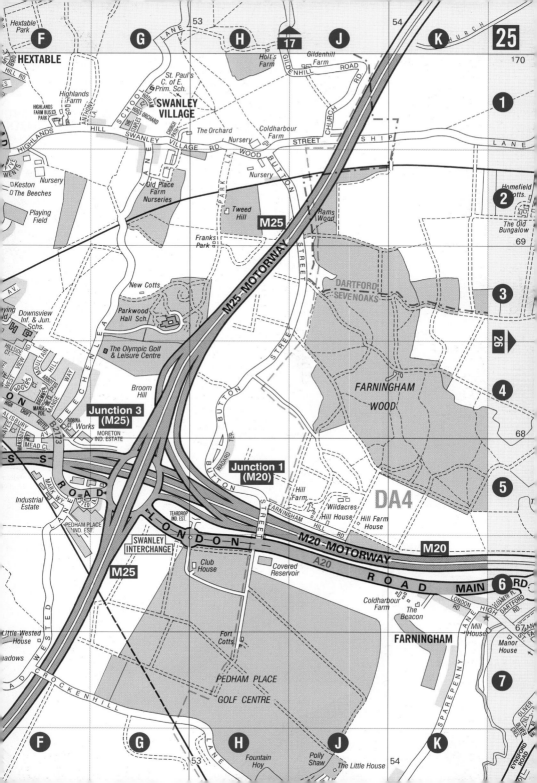

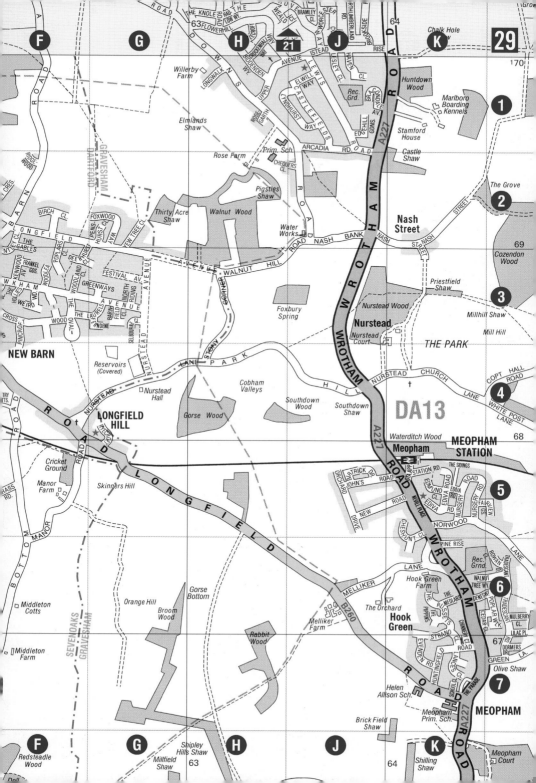

INDEX

Including Streets, Places & Areas, Hospitals & Hospices, Industrial Estates,
Selected Flats & Walkways, Junction Names and Selected Places of Interest.

HOW TO USE THIS INDEX

1. Each street name is followed by its Postal District (or, if outside the London Postal Districts, by its Posttown or Postal Locality), and then by its map reference; e.g. Abbey Gro. *SE2* ....4A **2** is in the South East 2 Postal District and is to be found in square 4A on page **2**. The page number is shown in bold type.

2. A strict alphabetical order is followed in which Av., Rd., St., etc. (though abbreviated) are read in full and as part of the street name; e.g. Apple Orchard appears after Applegarth Rd. but before Appleshaw Clo.

3. Streets and a selection of flats and walkways too small to be shown on the maps, appear in the index in *Italics* with the thoroughfare to which it is connected shown in brackets; e.g. *Alnwick Ct. Dart* ....6C **8** *(off Osbourne Rd.)*

4. Places and areas are shown in the index in **blue type** and the map reference is to the actual map square in which the town centre or area is located and not to the place name shown on the map; e.g. **Abbey Wood** 4A **2**

5. An example of a selected place of interest is **Beacon Wood Country Pk.** 4J **19**

6. An example of a hospital or hospice is **ARCHERY HOUSE** 6C **8**

GENERAL ABBREVIATIONS

All : Alley	Ct : Court	Lit : Little	Rd : Road
App : Approach	Cres : Crescent	Lwr : Lower	Shop : Shopping
Arc : Arcade	Cft : Croft	Mc : Mac	S : South
Av : Avenue	Dri : Drive	Mnr : Manor	Sq : Square
Bk : Back	E : East	Mans : Mansions	Sta : Station
Boulevd : Boulevard	Embkmt : Embankment	Mkt : Market	St. : Street
Bri : Bridge	Est : Estate	Mdw : Meadow	Ter : Terrace
B'way : Broadway	Fld : Field	M : Mews	Trad : Trading
Bldgs : Buildings	Gdns : Gardens	Mt : Mount	Up : Upper
Bus : Business	Gth : Garth	Mus : Museum	Va : Vale
Cvn : Caravan	Ga : Gate	N : North	Vw : View
Cen : Centre	Gt : Great	Pal : Palace	Vs : Villas
Chu : Church	Grn : Green	Pde : Parade	Vis : Visitors
Chyd : Churchyard	Gro : Grove	Pk : Park	Wlk : Walk
Circ : Circle	Ho : House	Pas : Passage	W : West
Cir : Circus	Ind : Industrial	Pl : Place	Yd : Yard
Clo : Close	Info : Information	Quad : Quadrant	
Comn : Common	Junct : Junction	Res : Residential	
Cotts : Cottages	La : Lane	Ri : Rise	

POSTTOWN AND POSTAL LOCALITY ABBREVIATIONS

Ash : Ash	*Fair* : Fairseat	*Hort K* : Horton Kirby	*S Dar* : South Darenth
B'hurst : Barnehurst	*F'ham* : Farningham	*Ist R* : Istead Rise	*S'fleet* : Southfleet
Bean : Bean	*Fawk* : Fawkham	*Knat* : Knatts Valley	*Stans* : Stansted
Belv : Belvedere	*Grav* : Gravesend	*Linf* : Linford	*Stne* : Stone
Bex : Bexley	*Grays* : Grays	*Long* : Longfield	*S at H* : Sutton At Hone
Bexh : Bexleyheath	*Grnh* : Greenhithe	*Long H* : Longfield Hill	*Swan* : Swanley
Blue : Bluewater	*G Str* : Green Street Green	*Meop* : Meopham	*Swans* : Swanscombe
Chst : Chislehurst	(Dartford)	*New Ash* : New Ash Green	*Til* : Tilbury
Cobh : Cobham	*Grn St* : Green Street Green	*N'fleet* : Northfleet	*Well* : Welling
Cray : Crayford	(Orpington)	*N Hth* : Northumberland Heath	*W King* : West Kingsdown
Crock : Crockenhill	*Hart* : Hartley	*Orp* : Orpington	*W Thur* : West Thurrock
Dart : Dartford	*Hawl* : Hawley	*St P* : St Pauls Cray	*Wilm* : Wilmington
E Til : East Tilbury	*Hex* : Hextable	*Sev* : Sevenoaks	
Eri : Erith	*High* : Higham	*Shorne* : Shorne	
Eyns : Eynsford	*Hods* : Hodsoll Street	*Sidc* : Sidcup	

A

Abbey Cres. *Belv* 4E **2**	Abbotswood Clo. *Belv* 3C **2**	Airedale Clo. *Dart* 1D **18**
Abbey Gro. *SE2* 4A **2**	Abbotts Clo. *SE28* 1A **2**	Alamein Gdns. *Dart* 7E **8**
Abbey Hill Rd. *Sidc* 2F **15**	Abbotts Clo. *Swan* 4F **25**	Alamein Rd. *Swans* 6A **10**
Abbey Mt. *Belv* 5D **2**	Abbott's Wlk. *Bexh* 7B **2**	Alanbrooke. *Grav* 7B **12**
Abbey Pl. *Dart* 5J **7**	Acacia Ct. *Grav* 7K **11**	Alan Clo. *Dart* 4H **7**
Abbey Rd. *Belv* 4B **2**	Acacia Rd. *Dart* 1J **17**	Alban Cres. *F'ham* 7B **26**
Abbey Rd. *Bexh* 4H **5**	Acacia Rd. *Grnh* 6F **9**	Albany Clo. *Bex* 7F **5**
Abbey Rd. *Grav* 1D **22**	Acacia Wlk. *Swan* 2C **24**	Albany Rd. *Belv* 6D **2**
Abbey Rd. *Grnh* 5K **9**	Acacia Way. *Sidc* 1C **14**	Albany Rd. *Bex* 7F **5**
Abbey Ter. *SE2* 4A **2**	Acorn Clo. *Chst* 5A **14**	Albany Rd. *Til* 1K **11**
Abbey Wood. 4A **2**	Acorn Ind. Est. *Dart* 5F **7**	Alberta Rd. *Eri* 1B **6**
Abbey Wood Camping &	Acorn Rd. *Dart* 5E **6**	Albert Murray Clo. *Grav* 7B **12**
Cvn. Site. *SE2* 4A **2**	Acworth Pl. *Dart* 6H **7**	Albert Rd. *Belv* 5D **2**
Abbey Wood Rd. *SE2* 4A **2**	Adams Sq. *Bexh* 3H **5**	Albert Rd. *Bex* 6K **5**
Abbots Fld. *Grav* 6B **22**	Adelaide Rd. *Til* 1J **11**	Albert Rd. *Dart* 3H **17**
	Admirals Wlk. *Grnh* 5J **9**	Albert Rd. *Swans* 6C **10**
	Agaton Rd. *SE9* 2A **14**	Albert Rd. Est. *Belv* 5D **2**
	Aintree Clo. *Grav* 3A **22**	Albion Pde. *Grav* 6C **12**

Albion Rd. *Bexh* 4J **5**
Albion Rd. *Grav* 7B **12**
Albion Ter. *Grav* 6B **12**
Albury Av. *Bexh* 2H **5**
Alconbury. *Bexh* 5A **6**
Alderman Clo. *Dart* 7D **6**
Alderney Rd. *Eri* 2J **3**
Alder Rd. *Sidc* 3C **14**
Alder Way. *Swan* 2C **24**
Alderwood Rd. *SE9* 6A **4**
Alers Rd. *Bexh* 5G **5**
Alexander Clo. *Sidc* 6B **4**
Alexander Rd. *Bexh* 2G **5**
Alexander Rd. *Grnh* 5K **9**
Alexandra Clo. *Swan* 2D **24**
Alexandra Rd. *Eri* 6K **3**
Alexandra Rd. *Grav* 7D **12**
Alexandra Rd. *Til* 2J **11**

Alfan La. *Dart* 5C **16**
Alford Rd. *Eri* 5G **3**
Alfred Ho. *Grav* 1J **21**
Alfred Pl. *N'fleet* 1J **21**
Alfred Rd. *Belv* 5D **2**
Alfred Rd. *Dart* 4K **17**
(in two parts)
Alfred Rd. *Grav* 2A **22**
Alfriston Clo. *Dart* 6D **6**
Alicia Ho. *Well* 1E **4**
Alkerden La. *Grnh & Swans* . .6K **9**
Allendale Clo. *Dart* 1E **18**
Allington Clo. *Grav* 1E **22**
All Saints Clo. *Swans* 5C **10**
All Saints Rd. *N'fleet* 1J **21**
Alma Rd. *Sidc* 3D **14**
Alma Rd. *Swans* 5C **10**
Alma, The. *Grav* 5E **22**
Almond Dri. *Swan* 2C **24**
Almond Rd. *Dart* 7D **8**
Alnwick Ct. *Dart* 6C **8**
(off Osbourne Rd.)
Alsike Rd. *SE2 & Eri* 3B **2**
Alton Clo. *Bex* 1H **15**
Amberley Ct. *Sidc* 5F **15**
Amberley Rd. *SE2* 6B **2**
Ambleside Rd. *Bexh* 2K **5**
Ambrooke Rd. *Belv* 3E **2**
Ambrose Clo. *Cray* 4E **6**
Ames Rd. *Swans* 6B **10**
Ampleforth Rd. *SE2* 2A **2**
Anchor Bay Ind. Est. *Eri* 1J **3**
Anchor Boulevd. *Dart* 4D **8**
Anchor Ct. *Eri* 7K **3**
Anderson Way. *Belv* 2G **3**
Andrew Clo. *Dart* 5C **6**
Andrews Pl. *Bex* 2D **16**
Anglesea Cen. *Grav* 6A **12**
Anglesea Pl. *Grav* 6A **12**
(off New Rd.)
Annandale Rd. *Sidc* 7B **4**
Anne Boleyn Ct. *SE9* 6A **4**
Anne of Cleeves Ct. *SE9* 6A **4**
Anne of Cleves Rd. *Dart* 5J **7**
Anstridge Path. *SE9* 6A **4**
Anstridge Rd. *SE9* 6A **4**
Anthony La. *Swan* 1F **25**
Anthony Rd. *Well* 1D **4**
Aperfield Rd. *Eri* 6K **3**
Appledore Av. *Bexh* 1B **6**
Appledore Cres. *Sidc* 3B **14**
Applegarth Dri. *Dart* 2K **17**
Applegarth Ho. *Eri* 2E **6**
Applegarth Rd. *SE28* 1A **2**
Apple Orchard. *Swan* 4C **24**
Appleshaw Clo. *Grav* 5K **21**
Appleton Clo. *Bexh* 2B **6**
Appleton Dri. *Dart* 3G **17**
Appold St. *Eri* 6K **3**
Apsledene. *Grav* 6C **22**
Arbuthnot La. *Bex* 6H **5**
Arcadian Av. *Bex* 6H **5**
Arcadian Clo. *Bex* 6H **5**
Arcadian Rd. *Bex* 6H **5**
Arcadia Rd. *Ist R* 1J **29**
Archer Way. *Swan* 2E **24**
ARCHERY HOUSE. 6C **8**
Arethusa Pl. *Grav* 4J **9**
Argali Ho. *Eri* 3C **2**
(off Kale Rd.)
Argles Clo. *Grnh* 5H **9**
Ariel Clo. *Grav* 4E **22**
Arkwright Rd. *Til* 2K **11**
Arlington Clo. *Sidc* 7B **4**
Armoury Dri. *Grav* 7B **12**
Arnold Pl. *Til* 1B **12**
Arnold Rd. *Grav* 2C **22**
Arnold's La. *S at H* 6A **18**
Arnott Clo. *SE28* 1A **2**
Arnsberga Way. *Bexh* 4K **5**
Arnside Rd. *Bexh* 1K **5**
Arran Clo. *Eri* 6H **3**
Artemis Clo. *Grav* 7D **12**
Arthur St. *Eri* 7K **3**
Arthur St. *Grav* 7K **11**
Arthur St. W. *Grav* 7K **11**
Artillery Row. *Grav* 7B **12**

Arundel Clo. *Bex* 6J **5**
Arundel Rd. *Dart* 4H **7**
Ascot Ct. *Bex* 7J **5**
Ascot Rd. *Grav* 3A **22**
Ash. 5H **31**
Ashbourne Av. *Bexh* 7C **2**
Ashburnham Rd. *Belv* 4G **3**
Ash Clo. *Sidc* 3E **14**
Ash Clo. *Swan* 2B **24**
Ashcroft Av. *Sidc* 6D **4**
Ashcroft Ct. *Dart* 7B **8**
Ashcroft Cres. *Sidc* 6D **4**
Ashdown Clo. *Bex* 7B **6**
Ashen Dri. *Dart* 7F **7**
Ashfield La. *Chst* 7A **14**
(in two parts)
Ash Ho. *New Ash* 2H **31**
Ashmore Gdns. *N'fleet* 3G **21**
Ashmore Gro. *Well* 3A **4**
Ash Rd. *Ash & New Ash* 4G **31**
Ash Rd. *Dart* 1J **17**
Ash Rd. *Grav* 4B **22**
Ash Rd. *Hawl* 4A **18**
Ash Rd. *Long & Hart* 3B **28**
Ash Tree Clo. *W King* 7C **30**
Ash Tree Dri. *W King* 7C **30**
Ashurst Clo. *Dart* 3E **6**
Ashwood Pl. *Bean* 3J **19**
Ashworth Av. *W King* 7A **30**
(off London Rd.)
Askern Clo. *Bexh* 4G **5**
Aspdin Rd. *N'fleet* 3G **21**
Aspen Clo. *Swan* 1C **24**
Aspen Ct. *Dart* 6B **8**
Aspen Grn. *Eri* 3D **2**
Aspen Ho. *Sidc* 3D **14**
Aston Clo. *Sidc* 3D **14**
Astor Rd. *W King* 6B **30**
Astra Dri. *Grav* 5D **22**
Athol Rd. *Eri* 5G **3**
Atlantic Clo. *Swans* 5B **10**
Atlas Rd. *Dart* 3A **8**
Attlee Dri. *Dart* 5B **8**
Attlee Rd. *SE28* 1A **2**
Auckland Clo. *Til* 2K **11**
Augustine Rd. *Grav* 7B **12**
(in two parts)
Austen Clo. *SE28* 1A **2**
Austen Clo. *Grnh* 6K **9**
Austen Clo. *Til* 2B **12**
Austen Gdns. *Dart* 4A **8**
Austen Rd. *Eri* 7F **3**
Austin Rd. *N'fleet* 1J **21**
Austral Clo. *Sidc* 3C **14**
Aveley Clo. *Eri* 6K **3**
Avenue Rd. *Belv* 4G **3**
Avenue Rd. *Bexh* 3H **5**
Avenue Rd. *Eri* 7G **3**
Avenue, The. *Bex* 7G **5**
Avenue, The. *Grav* 1K **21**
Avenue, The. *Grnh* 4J **9**
Avenue, The. *St P* 7E **14**
Avery Hill. 6A **4**
Avery Hill Rd. *SE9* 6A **4**
Avon Clo. *Grav* 2C **22**
Avondale Rd. *Well* 2F **5**
Avonmouth Rd. *Dart* 5J **7**
Awliscombe Rd. *Well* 2C **4**
Axminster Cres. *Well* 1F **5**
Axtane. *S'fleet* 7C **20**
Axtane Clo. *S at H* 1D **26**
Ayelands. *New Ash* 2H **31**
Ayelands La. *New Ash* 3H **31**
Azalea Dri. *Swan* 4C **24**

B

Back La. *Bex* 7K **5**
Back Rd. *Sidc* 4D **14**
Baden Powell Ho. *Belv* 3E **2**
(off Ambrooke Rd.)
Bader Wlk. *N'fleet* 3J **21**
Badlow Clo. *Eri* 7J **3**
Baker Beal Ct. *Bexh* 3A **6**
Bakerhill Clo. *N'fleet* 4J **21**
Bakers Av. *W King* 7B **30**

Balcombe Clo. *Bexh* 4G **5**
Baldwyn's Pk. *Bex* 2C **16**
Baldwyn's Rd. *Bex* 2C **16**
Balliol Rd. *Well* 2E **4**
Balmoral Gdns. *Bex* 7J **5**
Balmoral Rd. *S at H* 7C **18**
Baltimore Pl. *Well* 2C **4**
Banbury Vs. *S'fleet* 6C **20**
Banckside. *Hart* 4B **28**
Bank Ct. *Dart* 6K **7**
Bankside. *N'fleet* 6E **10**
Bankside Clo. *Bex* 4C **16**
Banks La. *Bexh* 4J **5**
Bank St. *Grav* 6A **12**
Banwell Rd. *Bex* 6G **5**
Barfield. *S at H* 7C **18**
Barham Clo. *Grav* 1E **22**
Barham Rd. *Dart* 7B **8**
Barnard Clo. *Chst* 7A **14**
Barnard Ct. *Dart* 6C **8**
(off Clifton Wlk.)
Barndale Ct. *Shorne* 5K **23**
Barnehurst. 3B **6**
Barnehurst Av. *Eri & Bexh* . . .1B **6**
Barnehurst Clo. *Eri* 1B **6**
Barnehurst Rd. *Bexh* 2B **6**
Barn End Dri. *Dart* 4H **17**
Barn End La. *Dart* 5H **17**
Barnes Cray. 4F **7**
Barnes Cray Rd. *Dart* 4F **7**
Barnett Clo. *Eri* 2E **6**
Barnfield. *Grav* 2K **21**
Barnfield Clo. *Grnh* 6G **9**
Barnfield Clo. *Long* 3G **29**
Barnfield Clo. *Swan* 7B **24**
Barnfield Rd. *Belv* 6D **2**
Barnock Clo. *Dart* 6D **6**
Barnwell Rd. *Dart* 3A **8**
Barrack Row. *Grav* 6A **12**
Barrington Rd. *Bexh* 2G **5**
Barr Rd. *Grav* 2E **22**
Barry Av. *Bexh* 7C **2**
Bartholomew Way. *Swan* 3D **24**
Bartlett Rd. *Grav* 1K **21**
Barton Clo. *Bexh* 5H **5**
Barton Rd. *Sidc* 6H **15**
Barton Rd. *S at H* 1C **26**
Bascombe Gro. *Dart* 6D **6**
Basilon Rd. *Bexh* 2H **5**
Basing Dri. *Bex* 6J **5**
Bath Rd. *Dart* 7G **7**
Bath St. *Grav* 6A **12**
Battle Rd. *Belv & Eri* 4G **3**
Baugh Rd. *Sidc* 5F **15**
Bayard Ct. *Bexh* 4A **6**
(off Watling St.)
Bayley Wlk. *SE2* 5C **2**
Bayly Rd. *Dart* 6B **8**
Baynham Clo. *Bex* 6J **5**
Baytree Clo. *Sidc* 1C **14**
Bazes Shaw. *New Ash* 2J **31**
(in two parts)
Beacon Dri. *Bean* 3J **19**
Beacon Rd. *Eri* 2K **3**
Beaconsfield Rd. *Bex* 2D **16**
Beacon Wood Country Pk.
. . . . .4J **19**
Beal Clo. *Well* 1D **4**
Bean. 3J **19**
Beane Cft. *Grav* 1E **22**
Bean Hill Cotts. *Grn St* 4J **19**
(in two parts)
Bean La. *Bean* 2J **19**
Bean Rd. *Bexh* 4G **5**
Bean Rd. *Grnh* 5J **9**
Beaton Clo. *Grnh* 5J **9**
Beatrice Gdns. *N'fleet* 2H **21**
Beaumont Dri. *N'fleet* 7H **11**
Beaverbank Rd. *SE9* 1A **14**
Beavers Lodge. *Sidc* 4C **14**
Beaverwood Rd. *Chst* 5B **14**
Beckett Clo. *Belv* 3D **2**
Becketts Clo. *Bex* 1B **16**
Beckley Clo. *Grav* 2G **23**
Becks Rd. *Sidc* 3D **14**
Becton Pl. *Eri* 7F **3**
Bedale Wlk. *Dart* 1C **18**

Bedens Rd. *Sidc* 6H **15**
Bedford Rd. *Dart* 7B **8**
Bedford Rd. *N'fleet* 2J **21**
Bedford Rd. *Sidc* 3B **14**
Bedford Sq. *Long* 3A **28**
Bedonwell Rd. *SE2 & Belv* . . .6C **2**
Bedonwell Rd. *Belv* 6C **2**
Bedonwell Rd. *Bexh* 1J **5**
Bedwell Rd. *Belv* 5E **2**
Beech Av. *Sidc* 7D **4**
Beech Av. *Swan* 4E **24**
Beech Ct. *Dart* 6B **8**
Beechcroft Av. *Bexh* 1C **6**
Beechenlea La. *Swan* 4F **25**
Beeches, The. *Swan* 7E **16**
Beeches, The. *Til* 2A **12**
Beechfield Rd. *Eri* 7J **3**
Beech Haven Ct. *Dart* 5C **6**
(off London Rd.)
Beechlands Clo. *Hart* 5D **28**
Beech Rd. *Dart* 1J **17**
Beech Wlk. *Dart* 4F **7**
Beechway. *Bex* 6G **5**
Beechwood Cres. *Bexh* 3G **5**
Beesfield La. *F'ham* 7B **26**
Beeston Ct. *Dart* 6C **8**
(off Hardwick Cres.)
Bell Clo. *Grnh* 5G **9**
Bellegrove Clo. *Well* 2C **4**
Bellegrove Pde. *Well* 3C **4**
Bellegrove Rd. *Well* 2A **4**
Bellevue Rd. *Bexh* 5J **5**
Bellman Av. *Grav* 1D **22**
Bellring Clo. *Belv* 6E **2**
Belmont Av. *Well* 2B **4**
Belmont La. *Chst* 5A **14**
(in two parts)
Belmont Rd. *Eri* 7E **2**
Beltana Dri. *Grav* 4D **22**
Belton Rd. *Sidc* 4D **14**
Beltwood Rd. *Belv* 4G **3**
Belvedere. 3F **3**
Belvedere Clo. *Grav* 1B **22**
Belvedere Ct. *Belv* 3D **2**
BELVEDERE PRIVATE CLINIC.
. . . . .5A **2**
Belvedere Rd. *SE2* 1A **2**
Belvedere Rd. *Bexh* 3J **5**
Benedict Clo. *Belv* 3C **2**
Benjamin Ct. *Belv* 6D **2**
Bennett Clo. *Well* 2D **4**
Bennett Ho. *Grav* 3J **21**
Bennett Way. *Dart* 4E **18**
Bentham Rd. *SE28* 1A **2**
Bentley Clo. *Long* 3F **29**
Bentley St. *Grav* 6B **12**
Bentley St. Ind. Est. *Grav* 6B **12**
Bere Clo. *Grnh* 5K **9**
Berens Ct. *Sidc* 4C **14**
Beresford Rd. *N'fleet* 7H **11**
Berkeley Av. *Bexh* 1G **5**
Berkeley Ct. *Swan* 3D **24**
Berkeley Cres. *Dart* 1A **18**
Berkhampstead Rd. *Belv* 5E **2**
Berkley Cres. *Grav* 6B **12**
Berkley Rd. *Grav* 6A **12**
Bermuda Rd. *Til* 2K **11**
Bernard St. *Grav* 6A **12**
Berrylands. *Hart* 6D **28**
Bertha Hollamby Ct. *Sidc* 5F **15**
(off Sidcup Hill)
Berwick Cres. *Sidc* 7B **4**
Berwick Rd. *Well* 1E **4**
Best Ter. *Swan* 6B **24**
Bethel Rd. *Well* 3F **5**
Betsham. 4C **20**
Betsham Rd. *Eri* 7K **3**
Betsham Rd. *S'fleet* 5A **20**
Betsham Rd. *Swans* 7B **10**
Betterton Dri. *Sidc* 2H **15**
Beult Rd. *Dart* 4F **7**
Bevan Pl. *Swan* 4E **24**
Bevans Clo. *Grnh* 6K **9**
Bevercote Wlk. *Belv* 6D **2**
Beverley Av. *Sidc* 7C **4**
Beverley Rd. *Bexh* 2B **6**
Bevis Clo. *Dart* 7D **8**

Bexley—Camdale Rd.

Bexley. 7K 5
Bexley Clo. *Dart* 5D 6
Bexley Cotts. *Hort K* 4C 26
Bexley Hall Place Vis. Cen. 6B 6
Bexleyheath. 4K 5
Bexley High St. *Bex* 7K 5
Bexley La. *Dart* 5D 6
Bexley La. *Sidc* 4F 15
Bexley Local Studies & Archive Cen. 6B 6 (Hall Place)
Bexley Rd. *SE9* 5A 4
Bexley Rd. *Eri* 1B 6 (in two parts)
Biddenden Way. *Ist R* 7H 21
Bideford Rd. *Well* 7A 2
Billet Hill. *Ash* 4F 31
Billings Hill Shaw. *Hart* 6C 28
Bilton Rd. *Eri* 2J 3
Binsey Wlk. *SE2* 2A 2
Birch Clo. *Long* 2F 29
Birches, The. *Swan* 2D 24
Birch Gro. *Well* 4D 4
Birchington Clo. *Bexh* 1A 6
Birch Pl. *Grnh* 6F 9
Birch Wlk. *Eri* 6G 3
Birchway. *W King* 7C 30
Birchwood Av. *Sidc* 2E 14
Birchwood Dri. *Dart* 4D 16
Birchwood Pde. *Dart* 4D 16
Birchwood Pk. Av. *Swan* 3D 24
Birchwood Rd. *Swan & Dart* 1B 24
Birkbeck Rd. *Sidc* 3D 14
Birling Rd. *Eri* 7H 3
Birtrick Dri. *Meop* 5J 29
Bishops Ct. *Grnh* 5G 9
Blackfen. 6D 4
Blackfen Pde. *Sidc* 6D 4
Blackfen Rd. *Sidc* 6B 4
Blackhorse Rd. *Sidc* 4D 14
Blackmans Clo. *Dart* 1H 17
Black Prince Interchange. (Junct.) 6A 6
Blackthorn Clo. *W King* 7C 30
Blackthorn Gro. *Bexh* 3H 5
Bladindon Dri. *Bex* 7F 5
Blair Clo. *Sidc* 5B 4
Blake Clo. *Well* 1B 4
Blake Gdns. *Dart* 4A 8
Blakemore Way. *Belv* 3C 2
Blake Way. *Til* 2B 12
Bleddyn Clo. *Sidc* 6F 5
Bledlow Clo. *SE28* 1A 2
Blendon. 6G 5
Blendon Dri. *Bex* 6G 5
Blendon Rd. *Bex* 6G 5
Blenheim Clo. *Dart* 6H 7
Blenheim Ct. *Sidc* 3A 14
Blenheim Dri. *Well* 1C 4
Blenheim Gro. *Grav* 7B 12
Blenheim Rd. *Dart* 6H 7
Blenheim Rd. *Sidc* 1F 15
Blewbury Ho. *SE2* 2B 2
Bligh Rd. *Grav* 6K 11
Blue Chalet Ind. Pk. *W King* 5A 30
Bluewater. 7G 9
Bluewater Parkway. *Blue* 7G 9
Bluewater Shop. Cen. *Grnh* 7G 9
Blyth Rd. *SE28* 1A 2
Bodle Av. *Swans* 7B 10
Boevey Path. *Belv* 5D 2
Bognor Rd. *Well* 1G 5
Boleyn Way. *Swans* 7B 10
Bonaventure Ct. *Grav* 4E 22
Bondfield Wlk. *Dart* 4A 8
Bonney Way. *Swan* 2D 24
Booth Clo. *SE28* 1A 2
Borland Clo. *Grnh* 5H 9
Bostall Hill. *SE2* 6A 2
Bostall La. *SE2* 4A 2
Bostall Mnr. Way. *SE2* 4A 2
Bostall Pk. Av. *Bexh* 7C 2
Bostall Rd. *Orp* 7E 14
Bosworth Ho. Eri 5J 3 (off Saltford Clo.)
Botany Rd. *N'fleet* 4D 10
Botsom La. *W King* 6A 30
Bott Rd. *Dart* 4A 18
Boucher Dri. *N'fleet* 3J 21
Boundary Houses. Grav 1J 21 (off Victoria Rd.)
Boundary Rd. *Sidc* 5B 4
Boundary St. *Eri* 7K 3
Bourne Ind. Pk., The. *Dart* 5D 6
Bourne Mead. *Bex* 5B 6
Bourne Pde. *Bex* 7A 6
Bourne Rd. *Bex & Dart* 7A 6
Bourne Rd. *Grav* 2E 22
Bourne Way. *Swan* 3B 24
Bow Arrow La. *Dart* 6B 8
Bower Rd. *Swan* 7F 17
Bowers Av. *N'fleet* 4J 21
Bowes Clo. *Sidc* 6E 4
Bowes Ct. Dart 6C 8 (off Osbourne Rd.)
Bowesden La. *Shorne* 7K 23
Bowes Wood. *New Ash* 3J 31
Bowford Av. *Bexh* 1H 5
Bowmans. 7E 6
Bowman's Rd. *Dart* 7E 6
Bown Clo. *Til* 3A 12
Bowness Rd. *Bexh* 2A 6
Boxgrove Rd. *SE2* 2A 2
Brabourne Cres. *Bexh* 6D 2
Brackendene. *Dart* 4D 16
Bracondale Av. *Ist R* 1J 29
BRACTON CENTRE, THE. 2E 16
Bracton La. *Bex* 2E 16
Bradbourne Rd. *Bex* 7K 5
Bradbury Ct. *Grav* 1J 21
Bradenham Av. *Well* 4D 4
Braemar Av. *Bexh* 4B 6
Braemar Gdns. *Sidc* 3A 14
Braeside Cres. *Bexh* 4B 6
Braesyde Clo. *Belv* 4D 2
Brakefield Rd. *S'fleet* 6E 20
Brakes Pl. *W King* 6B 30
Bramber Ct. Dart 6C 8 (off Bow Arrow La.)
Bramble Av. *Bean* 3K 19
Bramble Cft. *Eri* 4G 3
Brambledown. *Hart* 4C 28
Bramblefield Clo. *Long* 3A 28
Bramley Clo. *Ist R* 7J 21
Bramley Clo. *Swan* 4D 24
Bramley Ct. *Well* 1E 4
Bramley Pl. *Dart* 4F 7
Brampton Rd. *SE2 & Bexh* 6A 2
Brandon Rd. *Dart* 7B 8
Brandon St. *Grav* 7A 12
Brands Hatch Motor Racing Circuit. 5B 30
Brands Hatch Pk. *Fawk* 3C 30
Brands Hatch Rd. *Fawk* 4D 30
Bransell Clo. *Swan* 6B 24
Branton Rd. *Grnh* 6G 9
Brantwood Av. *Eri* 7G 3
Brantwood Rd. *Bexh* 2A 6
Brasted Clo. *Bexh* 5G 5
Brasted Rd. *Eri* 7J 3
Braundton Av. *Sidc* 1C 14
Braywood Rd. *SE9* 4A 4
Breakneck Hill. *Grnh* 5J 9
Bremner Clo. *Swan* 4F 25
Brenchley Av. *Grav* 5A 22
Brenda Ter. *Swans* 7B 10
Brendon Clo. *Eri* 1D 6
Brendon Rd. *SE9* 2A 14
Brennan Rd. *Til* 2A 12
Brent Clo. *Bex* 1H 15
Brent Clo. *Dart* 6C 8
Brentfield Rd. *Dart* 6B 8
Brentlands Dri. *Dart* 1B 18
Brent La. *Dart* 7A 8
Brent, The. *Dart* 7B 8
Brent Way. *Dart* 6C 8
Brewer's Fld. *Dart* 4H 17
Brewers Rd. *Shorne* 7H 23
Brewhouse Yd. *Grav* 6A 12
Briar Rd. *Bex* 3C 16
Briars, The. *W King* 6A 30
Briars Way. *Hart* 5D 28
Briary Ct. *Sidc* 5E 14
Brick Clo. *Eri* 6J 3
Brickfield Farm. *Long* 3D 28
Bridge Clo. *Dart* 3E 8
Bridge Ho. *Dart* 7K 7
Bridgen. 7H 5
Bridgen Rd. *Bex* 7H 5
Bridge Rd. *Bexh* 2H 5
Bridge Rd. *Eri* 2E 6
Bridges Dri. *Dart* 5C 8
Bright Clo. *Belv* 4B 2
Brightlands. *N'fleet* 4H 21
Brigstock Rd. *Belv* 4F 3
Brindle Ga. *Sidc* 1B 14
Brindley Clo. *Bexh* 3K 5
Brisbane Ho. *Til* 1K 11
Bristol Rd. *Grav* 3C 22
Bristow Rd. *Bexh* 1H 5
Britannia Dri. *Grav* 5E 22
Brittania Clo. *Eri* 6K 3
Brixham Rd. *Well* 1G 5
Broad Ditch Rd. *S'fleet* 7F 21
Broad La. *Dart* 4F 17
Broadoak Clo. *S at H* 6B 18
Broadoak Rd. *Eri* 7H 3
Broad Rd. *Swans* 6B 10
Broadway. *Bexh* 4H 5 (in three parts)
Broadway. *Swan* 6B 24
Broadway. *Til* 2J 11
Broadway Shop. Cen. *Bexh* 4K 5
Broadway Sq. *Bexh* 4K 5
Broadwood. *Grav* 5A 22
Bromley La. *Chst* 7A 14
Brompton Dri. *Eri* 2K 3
Bronte Clo. *Eri* 7F 3
Bronte Clo. *Til* 2B 12
Bronte Gro. *Dart* 4A 8
Bronte Vw. *Grav* 1B 22
Bronze Age Way. *Belv & Eri* 2F 3
Brookdale Rd. *Bex* 6H 5
Brooke Dri. *Grav* 1G 23
Brookend Rd. *Sidc* 1B 14
Brooklands. *Dart* 1K 17
Brooklands Av. *Sidc* 2A 14
Brook La. *Bex* 6G 5
Brook Pk. *Dart* 2B 18
Brook Rd. *N'fleet* 1H 21
Brook Rd. *Swan* 3C 24
Brookside Rd. *Ist R* 7J 21
Brook St. *Belv & Eri* 5F 3
Brook Va. *Eri* 1A 6
Broomfield Rd. *Bexh* 5K 5
Broomfield Rd. *Swans* 6B 10
Broomfields. *Hart* 5B 28
Broom Hill Ri. *Bexh* 5K 5
Broomhill Rd. *Dart* 6G 7
Broomhills. *S'fleet* 4B 20
Broom Mead. *Bexh* 6K 5
Broomwood Clo. *Bex* 2C 16
Brougham Ct. Dart 6C 8 (off Hardwick Cres.)
Browning Clo. *Well* 1B 4
Browning Rd. *Dart* 4A 8
Browning Wlk. *Til* 2B 12
Brown Rd. *Grav* 1D 22
Bruce Clo. *Well* 1E 4
Bruce Ct. *Sidc* 4C 14
Brummel Clo. *Bexh* 3B 6
Brunel Clo. *Til* 3A 12
Brunswick Clo. *Bexh* 4G 5
Brunswick Rd. *Bexh* 4G 5
Brunswick Wlk. *Grav* 7C 12 (in two parts)
Bryanston Rd. *Til* 2B 12
Buckingham Av. *Well* 4B 4
Buckingham Rd. *N'fleet* 7G 11
Buckles Ct. *Belv* 4B 2
Buckley Clo. *Dart* 2E 6
Bucks Cross Rd. *N'fleet* 3J 21
Buckthorn Ho. Sidc 3C 14 (off Longlands Rd.)
Buckwheat Ct. *Eri* 3B 2
Budleigh Cres. *Well* 1F 5
Bullace La. *Dart* 6K 7
Bull All. *Well* 3E 4
Bullbanks Rd. *Belv* 4G 3
Bullers Clo. *Sidc* 5H 15
Bull Hill. *Hort K* 4D 26
Bullivant Clo. *Grnh* 5H 9
Bull La. *Chst* 7A 14
Bulls Head Yd. Dart 6K 7 (off High St.)
Bull Yd. Grav 6A 12 (off Crooked La.)
Bunkers Hill. *Belv* 4E 2
Bunkers Hill. *Sidc* 3J 15
Burcharbro Rd. *SE2* 6B 2
Burch Rd. *N'fleet* 6J 11
Burdett Av. *Shorne* 4K 23
Burdett Clo. *Sidc* 5H 15
Burgate Clo. *Dart* 3E 6
Burghfield Rd. *Ist R* 7J 21
Burleigh Av. *Sidc* 5C 4
Burman Clo. *Dart* 7D 8
Burnaby Rd. *N'fleet* 7H 11
Burnell Av. *Well* 2D 4
Burnham Cres. *Dart* 4H 7
Burnham Rd. *Dart* 4H 7
Burnham Rd. *Sidc* 2H 15
Burnham Ter. *Dart* 5J 7
Burnham Trad. Est. *Dart* 4J 7
Burnley Rd. *Grays* 1G 9
Burns Av. *Sidc* 6E 4
Burns Clo. *Eri* 1E 6
Burns Clo. *Well* 1C 4
Burns Pl. *Til* 1A 12
Burnt Ho. La. *Dart* 4K 17 (in two parts)
Burnt Oak La. *Sidc* 6D 4
Burr Bank Ter. *Wilm* 4H 17
Burr Clo. *Bexh* 3J 5
Bursdon Clo. *Sidc* 2C 14
Bushfield Wlk. *Swans* 6B 10
Bushy Lees. *Sidc* 6C 4
Butchers Hill. *Shorne* 5K 23
Butcher's La. *New Ash* 2G 31
Butcher Wlk. *Swans* 7B 10
Butler's Pl. *Ash* 3H 31
Butterly Av. *Dart* 2A 18
Button St. *Swan* 2H 25
Buxton Rd. *Eri* 7H 3
Bycliffe M. *Grav* 7J 11
Bycliffe Ter. *Grav* 7J 11
Bynon Av. *Bexh* 3J 5
Byron Clo. *SE28* 1A 2
Byron Dri. *Eri* 7F 3
Byron Gdns. *Til* 1B 12
Byron Ho. *Dart* 5D 6
Byron Rd. *Dart* 4C 8

C

Cables Clo. *Belv* 3G 3
Cadogan Av. *Dart* 7E 8
Caerleon Clo. *Sidc* 5F 15
Cairns Clo. *Dart* 5J 7
Caithness Gdns. *Sidc* 6C 4
Calais Cotts. *Fawk* 2D 30
Calcroft Av. *Grnh* 5K 9
Calcutta Rd. *Til* 2J 11
Calderwood. *Grav* 5D 22
Caldy Rd. *Belv* 3F 3
Calfstock La. *F'ham* 4A 26
Caling Cft. *New Ash* 1J 31
Caliph Clo. *Grav* 3E 22
Callenders Cotts. *Belv* 2H 3
Calshot Ct. Dart 6C 8 (off Osbourne Rd.)
Calvert Clo. *Belv* 4E 2
Calvert Clo. *Sidc* 6H 15
Camborne Rd. *Sidc* 3F 15
Camborne Rd. *Well* 2B 4
Cambria Clo. *Sidc* 1A 14
Cambria Cres. *Grav* 4D 22
Cambria Ho. Eri 7J 3 (off Larner Rd.)
Cambrian Gro. *Grav* 7K 11
Cambridge Av. *Well* 4C 4
Cambridge Rd. *Sidc* 4B 14
Camdale Rd. *SE18* 1C 4

34 A-Z Dartford & Gravesend

Camden Clo. *Grav* 1F **21**
Camden Ct. *Belv* 5E **2**
Camden Rd. *Bex* 1J **15**
Cameron Clo. *Bex* 3D **16**
Campbell Rd. *Grav* 1J **21**
Campion Clo. *N'fleet* 4H **21**
Camrose Av. *Eri* 6F **3**
Canada Farm Rd.
 S Dar & Dart 4H **27**
Canada Rd. *Eri* 2K **3**
Canal Basin. *Grav* 6C **12**
Canal Ind. Pk. *Grav* 6C **12**
Canal Rd. *Grav* 6B **12**
Canberra Rd. *Bexh* 6B **2**
Canberra Sq. *Til* 2K **11**
Cannon Rd. *Bexh* 1H **5**
Canterbury Av. *Sidc* 2E **14**
Canterbury Clo. *Dart* 7B **8**
Canterbury Ho. *Eri* 7K **3**
Canterbury Rd. *Grav* 2B **22**
Canterbury Way. *W Thur* 1F **9**
Capelands. *New Ash* 2K **31**
Capel Pl. *Dart* 4H **17**
Capital Ind. Est. *Belv* 3F **3**
Capstan Cen. *Til* 1G **11**
Capstan Ct. *Dart* 4D **8**
Capstan M. *N'fleet* 7G **11**
Cardinal Clo. *Chst* 7A **14**
Carey Ct. *Bexh* 5A **6**
Carisbrooke Av. *Bex* 1G **15**
Carisbrooke Ct. Dart 6C **8**
 (off Osbourne Rd.)
Carl Ekman Ho. *Grav* 7G **11**
Carleton Pl. *Hort K* 4D **26**
Carleton Rd. *Dart* 7B **8**
Carlisle Rd. *Dart* 6B **8**
Carlton Av. *Grnh* 6F **9**
Carlton Grn. *Sidc* 4C **14**
Carlton Rd. *Eri* 6F **3**
Carlton Rd. *Sidc* 5C **14**
Carlton Rd. *Well* 3E **4**
Carlyle Rd. *SE28* 1A **2**
Carmelite Way. *Hart* 5C **28**
Carnet Clo. *Dart* 7D **6**
Carrack Ho. Eri 5J **3**
 (off Saltford Clo.)
Carr Ho. *Dart* 5D **6**
Carrill Way. *Belv* 4B **2**
Carrington Rd. *Dart* 6A **8**
Carsington Gdns. *Dart* 2J **17**
Carter Av. *W King* 7A **30**
Carters Row. *N'fleet* 1J **21**
Cartmel Rd. *Bexh* 1K **5**
Caspian Way. *Swans* 5B **10**
Casstine Clo. *Swan* 7E **16**
Castalia Ct. *Dart* 3A **8**
Castlefields. *Ist R* 1J **29**
Castle Hill. *Fawk & Hart* 5A **28**
Castle La. *Grav* 2G **23**
Castle Rd. *Swans* 6C **10**
Castle St. *Grnh* 5H **9**
Castle St. *Swans* 6C **10**
Castleton Av. *Bexh* 1C **6**
Catherine Howard Ct. *SE9* . . .6A **14**
Catherine of Aragon Ct.
 SE9 . . . . .6A **14**
Catherine Parr Ct. *SE9* 6A **14**
Cavell Cres. *Dart* 4B **8**
Cavendish Av. *Eri* 6G **3**
Cavendish Av. *Sidc* 7D **4**
Cavendish Av. *Well* 3C **4**
Cavendish Sq. *Long* 3B **28**
Caxton Clo. *Hart* 4C **28**
Cecil Rd. *Grav* 1J **21**
Cedar Av. *Grav* 4B **22**
Cedar Av. *Sidc* 7D **4**
Cedar Clo. *Meop* 6K **29**
Cedar Clo. *Swan* 2B **24**
Cedar Dri. *S at H* 2C **26**
Cedar Gro. *Bex* 6G **5**
Cedarhurst Cotts. *Bex* 7K **5**
Cedar Rd. *Dart* 1J **17**
Cedar Rd. *Eri* 1F **7**
Celia Av. W King 7B **30**
 (off London Rd.)
Centenary Ct. *F'ham* 7B **26**
Central Av. *Grav* 2A **22**

Central Av. *Til* 1K **11**
Central Av. *Well* 2C **4**
Central Pde. *Sidc* 3D **14**
Central Rd. *Dart* 4K **7**
Central Rd. *New Ash* 3H **31**
Centurion Way. *Eri* 3D **2**
Centuryan Pl. *Dart* 4G **7**
Cerne Rd. *Grav* 4D **22**
Cervia Way. *Grav* 3E **22**
Chadfields. *Til* 1K **11**
Chadwick Clo. *N'fleet* 2H **21**
Chalet Clo. *Bex* 4C **16**
Chalice Way. *Grnh* 5F **9**
Chalk. 2G **23**
Chalk Rd. *Grav* 1F **23**
Chalkstone Clo. *Well* 1D **4**
Chalky Bank. *Grav* 4K **21**
Challenge Clo. *Grav* 4E **22**
Chambers Clo. *Grnh* 5H **9**
Chancel Clo. *W King* 7B **30**
Chancelot Rd. *SE2* 4A **2**
Chancery Ct. *Dart* 7B **8**
Chandlers Dri. *Eri* 4H **3**
Chantry Av. *Hart* 6B **28**
Chantry Clo. *Sidc* 5H **15**
Chantry Ct. *Grav* 6B **12**
Chantry Heritage Cen., The.
 .6B **12**
Chapel Clo. *Dart* 5D **6**
Chapel Ct. *Swans* 6B **10**
Chapel Hill. *Dart* 5D **6**
Chapel Rd. *Bexh* 4K **5**
Chapel Wood. *New Ash* 1H **31**
 (in two parts)
Chapel Wood Rd.
 Ash & Hart 3H **31**
Chapman Rd. *Belv* 5F **3**
Chapman's La. *SE2 & Belv* . . .4A **2**
Charles Clo. *Sidc* 4E **14**
Charles Ct. *Eri* 6J **3**
Charles St. *Grnh* 5F **9**
Charlieville Rd. *Eri* 7G **3**
Charlotte Clo. *Bexh* 5H **5**
Charmouth Rd. *Well* 1F **5**
Charnock. *Swan* 4D **24**
 (in two parts)
Charter Dri. *Bex* 7H **5**
Charton Clo. *Belv* 6D **2**
Chartwell Clo. *SE9* 2A **14**
Chase Sq. *Grav* 6A **12**
Chase, The. *Bexh* 3A **6**
Chastilian Rd. *Dart* 7E **6**
Chatsworth Av. *Sidc* 1D **14**
Chatsworth Rd. *Dart* 5H **7**
Chaucer Clo. *Til* 2B **12**
Chaucer Pk. *Dart* 7A **8**
Chaucer Rd. *N'fleet* 3G **21**
Chaucer Rd. *Sidc* 1F **15**
Chaucer Rd. *Well* 1B **4**
Chaucer Way. *Dart* 4B **8**
 (in two parts)
Chave Rd. *Dart* 3K **17**
Chelsiter Ct. *Sidc* 4C **14**
Cheltenham Clo. *Grav* 5B **22**
Chenies, The. *Wilm* 4D **16**
Chequers Clo. *Ist R* 2H **29**
Cherry Av. *Swan* 4C **24**
Cherrydown Rd. *Sidc* 2G **15**
Cherry Tree La. *Dart* 3E **16**
Cherry Trees. *Hart* 5C **28**
Cherrywood Dri. *N'fleet* 4H **21**
Cheshunt Clo. *Meop* 5K **29**
Cheshunt Rd. *Belv* 5E **2**
Chessington Av. *Bexh* 7C **2**
Chesterfield Dri. *Dart* 5G **7**
Chester Rd. *Sidc* 5B **4**
 (in two parts)
Chesterton Way. *Til* 2B **12**
Chestnut Av. *Blue* 7G **9**
Chestnut Clo. *N'fleet* 6J **11**
Chestnut Clo. *Sidc* 1D **14**
Chestnut Dri. *Bexh* 4C **6**
Chestnut Gro. *Dart* 4C **16**
Chestnut Rd. *Dart* 1J **17**
Cheswick Clo. *Dart* 4E **6**
Chesworth Clo. *Eri* 2D **6**
Chevenings, The. *Sidc* 3F **15**

Cheviot Clo. *Bexh* 2D **6**
Cheviot Ho. Grav 6G **11**
 (off Laburnum Gro.)
Cheyne Wlk. *Long* 3B **28**
Chichester Ri. *Grav* 4C **22**
Chichester Rd. *Grnh* 6G **9**
Chichester Wharf. *Eri* 5J **3**
Chiddingstone Av. *Bexh* 7D **2**
Chieveley Pde. Bexh 4A **6**
 (off Chieveley Rd.)
Chieveley Pde. *Bexh* 3A **6**
 (Mayplace Rd. E.)
Chieveley Rd. *Bexh* 4A **6**
Chiffinch Gdns. *N'fleet* 3H **21**
Childs Cres. *Swans* 6A **10**
Chilham Clo. *Bex* 7J **5**
Chiltern Clo. *Bexh* 1D **6**
Chiltern Rd. *N'fleet* 3H **21**
Chinnery Ct. *Meop* 6K **29**
Chipstead Rd. *Eri* 7J **3**
Chislehurst. 7A **14**
Chislehurst Rd. *Sidc* 5D **14**
Christchurch Av. *Eri* 6H **3**
Christ Chu. Cres. *Grav* 7B **12**
Christchurch Rd. *Dart* 7H **7**
Christchurch Rd. *Grav* 1B **22**
Christchurch Rd. *Sidc* 4C **14**
Christchurch Rd. *Til* 1K **11**
Christian Fields. 4C **22**
Christian Fields Av. *Grav* 4B **22**
Christopher Clo. *Sidc* 5C **4**
Christopher Ho. Sidc 2D **14**
 (off Station Rd.)
Chudleigh. *Sidc* 4E **14**
Church All. Grav 6A **12**
 (off Princes St.)
Church Av. *Sidc* 5D **14**
Church Farm Clo. *Swan* 6B **24**
Church Fld. *Dart* 2J **17**
Churchfield Rd. *Well* 3D **4**
Church Hill. *Cray* 4D **6**
Church Hill. *Dart* 2J **17**
Church Hill. *Eri* 5F **9**
Churchill Clo. *Dart* 1C **18**
Churchill Pk. *Dart* 5B **8**
Churchill Rd.
 Grav & N'fleet 1J **21**
Churchill Rd. *Hort K* 4D **26**
Church La. *Chst* 7A **14**
Church La. *Grav* 3H **23**
Church Manorway. *Eri* 3H **3**
Church Path. *Grnh* 5G **9**
Church Path. *N'fleet* 6F **11**
Church Path. *Swan* 1G **25**
Church Rd. *Ash* 5H **31**
Church Rd. *Bexh* 2J **5**
Church Rd. *E Til* 1J **11**
Church Rd. *Eri* 5H **3**
Church Rd. *Grav & Cobh* 6B **22**
Church Rd. *Grnh* 5G **9**
Church Rd. *Hart* 5C **28**
Church Rd. *New Ash* 2J **31**
Church Rd. *Sidc* 4D **14**
Church Rd. *S at H* 6A **18**
 (in two parts)
Church Rd. *Swan* 7C **24**
 (Crockenhill)
Church Rd. *Swan* 1J **25**
 (Swanley Village)
Church Rd. *Swans* 6C **10**
Church Rd. *Well* 2E **4**
Church Rd. *W King* 7B **30**
Church Row. *Chst* 7A **14**
Church Row M. *Chst* 7A **14**
Church St. *Grav* 6A **12**
Church St. *S'fleet* 5D **20**
Church Trad. Est. *Eri* 7K **3**
Church Vw. *Swan* 3C **24**
Church Wlk. *Dart* 3J **17**
Church Wlk. *Grav* 1C **22**
 (in two parts)
Chyngton Clo. *Sidc* 3C **14**
Cimba Wood. *Grav* 4D **22**
Circle, The. *Til* 1K **11**
Cirrus Cres. *Grav* 5D **22**
Civic Sq. *Til* 2K **11**
Claire Causeway. *Dart* 4F **9**

Claremont Cres. *Dart* 4D **6**
Claremont Pl. Grav 7A **12**
 (off Arthur St.)
Claremont Rd. *Swan* 7D **16**
Clarence Cres. *Sidc* 3E **14**
Clarence Pl. *Grav* 7A **12**
Clarence Rd. *Bexh* 4H **5**
Clarence Rd. *Sidc* 3E **14**
Clarence Row. *Grav* 7A **12**
Clarenden Pl. *Dart* 5D **16**
Clarendon Gdns. *Dart* 7E **8**
Clarendon M. *Bex* 1A **16**
Clarendon Rd. *Grav* 6B **12**
Clare Way. *Bexh* 1H **5**
Clark Clo. *Eri* 1F **7**
Claston Clo. *Dart* 4D **6**
Clay Farm Rd. *SE9* 2A **14**
Clayton Cft. Rd. *Dart* 2F **17**
Claywood La. *Bean* 3A **20**
Clayworth Clo. *Sidc* 6E **4**
Clearways Bus. Est.
 W King 7A **30**
Clearways Cvn. Pk.
 W King 7A **30**
Cleeve Pk. Gdns. *Sidc* 2E **14**
Cleeves Vw. Dart 6J **7**
 (off Priory Pl.)
Clement Street. 6J **17**
Clement St.
 Swan & S at H 6J **17**
Cleveland Ho. *Grav* 6G **11**
Cleveland Rd. *Well* 2C **4**
Cleve Rd. *Sidc* 3G **15**
Cleves Ct. *Dart* 7K **7**
Clewer Ho. SE2 . . . . .2B **2**
 (off Wolvercote Rd.)
Cliff Reach. *Blue* 6G **9**
Clifton Gro. *Grav* 7A **12**
Clifton Marine Pde. *Grav* 6J **11**
Clifton Rd. *Grav* 6K **11**
Clifton Rd. *Sidc* 4B **14**
Clifton Rd. *Well* 3F **5**
Clifton Wlk. *Dart* 6C **8**
Clinton Av. *Well* 4D **4**
Clipper Boulevd. *Dart* 4F **9**
Clipper Boulevd. W. *Dart* 3E **8**
Clipper Cres. *Grav* 4E **22**
Clive Av. *Dart* 6E **6**
Clive Rd. *Belv* 4E **2**
Clive Rd. *Grav* 6A **12**
Cloisters Ct. *Bexh* 3A **6**
Cloisters, The. Dart 6K **7**
 (off Orchard St.)
Close, The. *Bex* 6K **5**
Close, The. *Long* 2E **28**
Close, The. *Sidc* 4E **14**
Close, The. *Wilm* 3H **17**
Cloudesley Rd. *Bexh* 1J **5**
Cloudesley Rd. *Eri* 1E **6**
Clovelly Rd. *Bexh* 6C **2**
Cloverdale Gdns. *Sidc* 6C **4**
Clovers, The. *N'fleet* 4H **21**
Clydesdale Ho. *Eri* 2C **2**
 (off Kale Rd.)
Clydon Clo. *Eri* 6J **3**
Coalhouse Fort. 1J **13**
Cob Dri. *Shorne* 5K **23**
Cobham Clo. *Grnh* 6J **9**
Cobham Clo. *Sidc* 6E **4**
Cobham Ho. *Eri* 7K **3**
Cobham Pl. *Bexh* 5G **5**
Cobham St. *Grav* 7K **11**
Cobham Ter. *Grnh* 6J **9**
Cobham Ter. N'fleet 1J **21**
 (off Southfleet Rd.)
Cobsdene. *Grav* 6C **22**
Cocksure La. *Sidc* 3K **15**
Codrington Cres. *Grav* 5B **22**
Codrington Gdns. *Grav* 5C **22**
 (in two parts)
Coldblow. 1B **16**
Cold Blow Cres. *Bex* 1C **16**
Coldharbour Rd. *N'fleet* 2H **21**
Colebeck St. *Eri* 6K **3**
Colebrooke Ct. Sidc 4E **14**
 (off Granville Rd.)
Cole Clo. *SE28* 1A **2**

Coleman Rd.—Dickens Clo.

Coleman Rd. Belv 4E 2
Colepits Wood Rd. SE9 5A 4
Coleridge Rd. Dart 4C 8
Coleridge Rd. Til 2B 12
Colin Clo. Dart 6C 8
College Rd. N'fleet 5E 10
College Rd. Swan 1D 24
Coller Cres. Dart 5F 19
Collindale Av. Eri 7F 3
Collindale Av. Sidc 1D 14
Collington Clo. N'fleet 7H 11
Collingwood Ho. Grnh 5K 9
Colney Rd. Dart 6A 8
Coltstead. New Ash 2H 31
Columbus Ct. Eri 7K 3
Columbus Sq. Eri 6K 3
Colyer Rd. N'fleet 2F 21
Colyers Clo. Eri 1C 6
Colyers La. Eri 1B 6
Colyers Wlk. Eri 1D 6
Colyton Clo. Well 1G 5
Combeside. SE18 1C 4
Commercial Pl. Grav 6B 12
Common La. Dart 2F 17
Commonwealth Way. SE2 5A 2
Compton Pl. Eri 6K 3
Conference Rd. SE2 4A 2
Congress Rd. SE2 4A 2
Conifer Av. Hart 6B 28
Conifer Way. Swan 1B 24
Conisborough Ct. Dart 6C 8
(off Osbourne Rd.)
Coniston Av. Well 3B 4
Coniston Clo. Bexh 1B 6
Coniston Clo. Dart 1G 17
Coniston Clo. Eri 7J 3
Coniston Rd. Bexh 1B 6
Constable Rd. N'fleet 3H 21
Constitution Cres. Grav 1B 22
(off Constitution Hill)
Constitution Hill. Grav 1B 22
Consul Gdns. Swan 7F 17
Cook Ct. Eri 7K 3
Cookham Rd.
Swan 7K 15 & 2A 24
Cookson Gro. Eri 7F 3
Cook Sq. Eri 7K 3
Coombe Rd. Grav 2B 22
Coombfield Dri. Dart 4E 18
Cooper Clo. Grnh 5G 9
Coopers Clo. S Dar 1E 26
Coopers Rd. N'fleet 1J 21
Coopers Rd. Swans 7C 10
Coote Rd. Bexh 1J 5
Copper Beech Clo. Grav 7C 12
Copperfield Clo. Grav 1F 23
Copperfields Shop. Cen.
Dart 6K 7
Copperfield Way. Chst 6A 14
Coppice, The. Bex 3C 16
Copse Side. Hart 3B 28
Copsewood Clo. Sidc 6B 4
Coptefield Dri. Belv 3B 2
Copt Hall Rd. Cobh 4K 29
Coralline Wlk. SE2 2A 2
Corbylands Rd. Sidc 7B 4
Corhaven Ho. Eri 7J 3
Corinthian Manorway. Eri 4H 3
Corinthian Rd. Eri 4H 3
Cornel Ho. Sidc 3D 14
Cornelia Pl. Eri 6J 3
Cornell Clo. Sidc 6H 15
Cornwall Av. Well 3B 4
Cornwall Dri. Orp 7F 15
Cornwallis Av. SE9 2A 14
Cornwallis Clo. Eri 6K 3
Cornwall Rd. Dart 3A 8
Cornwell Av. Grav 3B 22
Coronation Clo. Bex 6G 5
Coronation Ct. Eri 7H 3
Cortland Clo. Dart 6D 6
Cotleigh Av. Bex 2G 15
Coton Rd. Well 3D 4
Cotswold Clo. Bexh 2D 6
Cotswold Rd. N'fleet 3H 21
Cottage Fld. Clo. Sidc 1F 15
Cotton La. Dart & Grnh 5D 8
Coulter Ho. Grnh 5K 9
Coulton Av. N'fleet 7H 11
Council Av. N'fleet 6F 11
Court Av. Belv 5D 2
Court Cres. Swan 4D 24
Courtleet Dri. Eri 1A 6
Court Lodge. Belv 5E 2
Court Lodge. Shorne 6K 23
Court Rd. Dart 5F 19
Coutts Av. Shorne 4K 23
Cowdrey Ct. Dart 7G 7
Cowley Av. Grnh 5G 9
Cowper Av. Til 1A 12
Cowper Clo. Well 5D 4
Cowper Rd. Belv 4D 2
Crabtree Manorway N.
Belv 2G 3
Crabtree Manorway S.
Belv 3G 3
Cradley Rd. SE9 1A 14
Cramonde Ct. Well 2D 4
Cranbrook Ho. Eri 7K 3
(off Boundary St.)
Cranbrook Rd. Bexh 1J 5
Cranford Rd. Dart 1K 17
Cranleigh Clo. Bex 6A 6
Cranleigh Dri. Swan 4D 24
Crawfords. Swan 7D 16
Crawley Ct. Grav 6K 11
Craybrooke Rd. Sidc 4E 14
Crayburne. S'fleet 5C 20
Cray Clo. Dart 4F 7
Craydene Rd. Eri 1E 6
Crayford. 5D 6
Crayford Greyhound Stadium. 6D 6
Crayford High St. Dart 4D 6
Crayford Ind. Est. Cray 5E 6
Crayford Rd. Cray 5E 6
Crayford Way. Dart 5E 6
Craylands La. Swans 5A 10
Craylands Sq. Swans 5A 10
Craymill Sq. Dart 2E 6
Cray Rd. Belv 6E 2
Cray Rd. Dart 4F 7
Cray Rd. Sidc 6F 15
Cray Rd. Swan 6A 24
Crayside Ind. Est. Dart 4G 7
Creek, The. Grav 5E 10
Cremorne Rd. N'fleet 7J 11
Crescent Gdns. Swan 2B 24
Crescent Rd. Eri 6K 3
Crescent Rd. Sidc 3C 14
Crescent, The. Bex 7F 5
Crescent, The. Grnh 5K 9
Crescent, The. Long 3B 28
Crescent, The. N'fleet 2J 21
Crescent, The. Sidc 4C 14
Crest Vw. Grnh 4H 9
Crete Hall Rd. Grav 6G 11
Crichton Ho. Sidc 6G 15
Cricketers Clo. Eri 5J 3
Crittall's Corner. (Junct.) 7E 14
Crockenhall Way. Ist R 7H 21
Crockenhill. 6C 24
Crockenhill La. Eyns 7F 25
Crockenhill Rd.
Orp & Swan 6A 24
Croft Clo. Belv 5D 2
Crofton Av. Bex 7G 5
Croft, The. Swan 3B 24
Croft Way. Sidc 3B 14
Crombie Rd. Sidc 1A 14
Cromwell Lodge. Bexh 5H 5
Crooked La. Grav 6A 12
Crook Log. Bexh 3G 5
Cross La. Bex 7J 5
Cross La. E. Grav 2A 22
Cross La. W. Grav 2A 22
Crossness Footpath. Eri 1D 2
Crossness La. SE28 1B 2
Cross Rd. Dart 6H 7
Cross Rd. Hawl 4A 18
Cross Rd. N'fleet 6J 11
Cross Rd. Sidc 4E 14
Cross St. Eri 6J 3
Cross St. Grav 6A 12
Crossway. SE28 1A 2
Crossways. Dart 4D 8
Crossways Boulevd.
Dart 4D 8
Crossways 25 Bus. Pk.
Dart 4D 8
Crowden Way. SE28 1A 2
Crowhurst La. Ash 7D 30
Crown Ct. Til 2K 11
Crown Grn. Shorne 5K 23
Crown La. Shorne 4K 23
Crown Woods Way. SE9 5A 4
Croxley Grn. Orp 7E 14
Croyde Clo. Sidc 7A 4
Cruden Rd. Grav 3E 22
Crumpsall St. SE2 4A 2
Crusader Ct. Dart 5A 8
Crusoe Rd. Eri 5H 3
Cugley Rd. Dart 7D 8
Culcroft. Hart 3C 28
Culvey Clo. Hart 5B 28
Cumberland Av. Grav 7B 12
Cumberland Av. Well 3B 4
Cumberland Ct. Well 2B 4
Cumberland Dri. Bexh 7C 2
Cumberland Dri. Dart 7A 8
Cumbrian Av. Bexh 2D 6
Curates Wlk. Dart 3J 17
Curlews, The. Grav 2C 22
Curran Av. Sidc 5C 4
Cutmore St. Grav 7A 12
Cuxton Clo. Bexh 5H 5
Cyclamen Rd. Swan 4C 24
Cygnet Gdns. N'fleet 2J 21
Cypress Tree Clo. Sidc 1C 14
Cyril Lodge. Sidc 4D 14
Cyril Rd. Bexh 2H 5

D

Dabbling Clo. Eri 1K 3
Dahlia Dri. Swan 2E 24
Dahlia Rd. SE2 5A 2
Dairy Clo. S at H 7C 18
Dalberg Way. SE2 3B 2
Dale Clo. Dart 6E 6
Dale End. Dart 6E 6
Dale Rd. Dart 6E 6
Dale Rd. S'fleet 4D 20
Dale Rd. Swan 2B 24
Dale Vw. Eri 2E 6
Dale Wlk. Dart 1D 18
Dallin Rd. Bexh 4G 5
Dalmeny Rd. Eri 1A 6
Daltons Rd. Orp & Swan 7B 24
Damigos Rd. Grav 1E 22
Damon Clo. Sidc 3E 14
Damson Ct. Swan 4C 24
Dane Clo. Bex 7K 5
Danehill Wlk. Sidc 3D 14
Danes Clo. N'fleet 3F 21
Dansington Rd. Well 4D 4
Danson Cres. Well 3D 4
Danson Interchange.
(Junct.) 5F 5
Danson La. Well 4E 4
Danson Mead. Well 3F 5
Danson Rd. Bex & Bexh 6F 5
(in two parts)
Danson Underpass. Sidc 6F 5
(in two parts)
Darenth. 5D 18
Darenth Dri. Grav 1G 23
Darenth Hill. Dart 5D 18
Darenth Interchange.
(Junct.) 3B 18
Darenth Park Av. Dart 2E 18
Darenth Rd. Dart 7A 8
Darenth Rd. Hawl 4C 18
Darenth Rd. Well 1D 4
Darenth Wood Rd. Dart 4F 19
(in two parts)
Darent Mead. S at H 1C 26
DARENT VALLEY HOSPITAL. 1F 19
Darlton Clo. Dart 3E 6
Darnley Ct. Grav 7K 11
(off Darnley Rd.)
Darnley Rd. Grav 1K 21
(in two parts)
Darnley St. Grav 7K 11
Darns Hill. Swan 7B 24
Dartford. 6K 7
Dartford Borough Mus. 7K 7
Dartford By-Pass.
Bex & Dart 7C 6
Dartford Heath. (Junct.) 1D 16
Dartford River Crossing.
Dart & Grays 2F 9
Dartford Rd. Bex 1B 16
Dartford Rd. Dart 6F 7
Dartford Rd.
F'ham & Hort K 6A 26
(in two parts)
Dartford Trade Pk. Dart 2K 17
Dartford Tunnel.
Dart & Grays 3E 8
Dartford Tunnel App. Rd.
Dart 7C 8
Darwin Rd. Til 1J 11
Darwin Rd. Well 3C 4
Dashwood Clo. Bexh 5K 5
Dashwood Rd. Grav 1K 21
Davenport Rd. Sidc 2H 15
David Coffer Ct. Belv 4F 3
David Ho. Sidc 3D 14
Davis Av. N'fleet 1H 21
Davy's Pl. Grav 6D 22
Dawes Clo. Grnh 5G 9
Dawson Dri. Swan 7D 16
Days La. Sidc 7B 4
Dean Bottom. 3J 27
Debrabant Clo. Eri 6H 3
Deepdene Rd. Well 3D 4
Deerhurst Clo. Long 3F 29
Defoe Clo. Eri 1D 6
Deirdre Chapman Ho.
Swans 6B 10
(off Craylands La.)
Dell, The. Bex 1D 16
Dell, The. Grnh 5J 9
De Luci Rd. Eri 5G 3
De Lucy St. SE2 4A 2
Denberry Dri. Sidc 3E 14
Dene Av. Sidc 7E 4
Dene Clo. Dart 4D 16
Dene Dri. Long 2E 28
Dene Holm Rd. N'fleet 3G 21
Dene Rd. Dart 7A 8
Denesway. Meop 6K 29
Dene Wlk. Long 3B 28
Denham Clo. Well 3F 5
Deniston Av. Bex 1H 15
Dennis Rd. Grav 3K 21
Denny Ct. Dart 6C 8
(off Bow Arrow La.)
Denton. 7D 12
Denton Cvn. Site. Grav 7E 12
Denton Ct. Rd. Grav 7D 12
Denton Rd. Bex 2D 16
Denton Rd. Dart 7D 6
Denton Rd. Well 7A 2
Denton St. Grav 7D 12
Denton Ter. Bex 2D 16
Denver Rd. Dart 7F 7
Dering Way. Grav 1E 22
Derwent Clo. Dart 1G 17
Derwent Cres. Bexh 2K 5
Detling Rd. Eri 7H 3
Detling Rd. N'fleet 1G 21
Devon Ct. S at H 1C 26
Devon Rd. S Dar 1C 26
Devonshire Av. Dart 6G 7
Devonshire Rd. Bexh 4H 5
Devonshire Rd. Grav 1A 22
Dewlands Av. Dart 7C 8
Dexter Ho. Eri 3C 2
(off Kale Rd.)
Dial Clo. Grnh 5K 9
Diana Ct. Eri 6J 3
Dickens Av. Dart 4B 8
Dickens Av. Til 1A 12
Dickens Clo. Eri 7F 3

36 A-Z Dartford & Gravesend

Dickens Clo. *Hart* 5C **28**
Dickens Dri. *Chst* 6A **14**
Dickens Rd. *Grav* 1D **22**
Disraeli Clo. *SE28* 1A **2**
Ditton Rd. *Bexh* 5G **5**
Dobson Rd. *Grav* 5D **22**
Dock Rd. *Grays* 1H **11**
Dock Rd. *Til* 1H **11**
Dogwood Clo. *N'fleet* 4J **21**
Dolphin Yd., The. *Grav* 6A **12**
(off Queen St.)
Donald Biggs Dri. *Grav* 7C **12**
Donnington Ct. *Dart* 6C **8**
(off Bow Arrow La.)
Dorchester Av. *Bex* 1G **15**
Dorchester Clo. *Dart* 7A **8**
Dorchester Clo. *Orp* 7E **14**
Dorchester Rd. *Grav* 3C **22**
Dorcis Av. *Bexh* 2H **5**
Doria Dri. *Grav* 3D **22**
Doris Av. *Eri* 1B **6**
Dormers Dri. *Meop* 7K **29**
Dorothy Evans Clo. *Bexh* 4A **6**
Dorrit Way. *Chst* 6A **14**
Dorset Av. *Well* 4C **4**
Dorset Cres. *Grav* 4D **22**
Dothill Rd. *SE18* 1A **4**
Douglas Rd. *Well* 1E **4**
Dovedale Clo. *Well* 2D **4**
Dovedale Rd. *Dart* 1D **18**
Dover Rd. *N'fleet* 7G **11**
Dover Rd. E. *Grav* 7H **11**
Dowding Wlk. *N'fleet* 3H **21**
Dowling Ho. *Belv* 3D **2**
Downage, The. *Grav* 2K **21**
Downbank Av. *Bexh* 1C **6**
Downe Clo. *Well* 7A **2**
Downs Av. *Dart* 7B **8**
Downs Hill. *S'fleet* 7F **21**
Downs Rd. *Ist R* 4G **21**
Downs Valley. *Hart* 4B **28**
Downsview Clo. *Swan* 3E **24**
Doyle Clo. *Eri* 1D **6**
Doyle Way. *Til* 2B **12**
Drake Ct. *Eri* 7K **3**
(off Frobisher Rd.)
Draper Clo. *Belv* 4D **2**
Drive, The. *Bex* 6F **5**
Drive, The. *Eri* 7F **3**
Drive, The. *Grav* 4C **22**
Drive, The. *Long* 3E **28**
Drive, The. *Sidc* 3E **14**
Drove Way, The. *Grav* 7H **21**
Drudgeon Way. *Bean* 3J **19**
Drummond Clo. *Eri* 1D **6**
Dryden Pl. *Til* 1A **12**
Dryden Rd. *Well* 1C **4**
Dryhill Rd. *Belv* 6D **2**
Ducketts Rd. *Dart* 5E **6**
Dudley Rd. *N'fleet* 7H **11**
Dudsbury Rd. *Dart* 6G **7**
Dudsbury Rd. *Sidc* 6E **14**
Dukes Orchard. *Bex* 1B **16**
Dulverton Rd. *SE9* 2A **14**
Duncroft. *SE18* 1B **4**
Dunkin Rd. *Dart* 4B **8**
Dunkirk Clo. *Grav* 5B **22**
Dunlop Rd. *Til* 1J **11**
Dunstall Welling Est. *Well* . . .2E **4**
Dunwich Rd. *Bexh* 1J **5**
Durant Rd. *Swan* 6F **17**
Durham Rd. *Sidc* 5E **14**
Duriun Way. *Eri* 2K **3**
Durndale La. *N'fleet* 4H **21**
(in two parts)
Durrant Way. *Swans* 7B **10**
Duxford Ho. *SE2* 2B **2**
(off Wolvercote Rd.)
Dykewood Clo. *Bex* 3C **16**
Dylan Rd. *Belv* 3E **2**

E

Eagles Rd. *Grnh* 4H **9**
Eagle Way. *N'fleet* 5D **10**
Eardemont Clo. *Dart* 4E **6**
Eardley Rd. *Belv* 5E **2**
Earl Rd. *N'fleet* 2H **21**
Eastcote Rd. *Well* 2A **4**
East Cres. Rd. *Grav* 6B **12**
Eastern Ind. Est. *Eri* 2E **2**
Eastern Way. *SE28* 2A **2**
East Hill. *Dart* 7A **8**
East Hill. *S Dar* 1D **26**
East Holme. *Eri* 1C **6**
E. Kent Av. *N'fleet* 6F **11**
East La. *S Dar* 2E **26**
Eastleigh Rd. *Bexh* 3B **6**
East Mill. *Grav* 6J **11**
E. Milton Rd. *Grav* 7C **12**
East Rd. *Well* 2E **4**
E. Rochester Way.
Sidc & Bex 4B **4**
Eastry Rd. *Eri* 7E **2**
East St. *Bexh* 4K **5**
East Ter. *Grav* 6B **12**
East Ter. *Sidc* 1B **14**
East Wickham. 1F **5**
East Woodside. *Bex* 1H **15**
Eaton Rd. *Sidc* 2G **15**
Eaton Sq. *Long* 3A **28**
Ebbsfleet Ind. Est. *N'fleet* . . .5D **10**
Ebbsfleet Wlk. *N'fleet* 6E **10**
Echo Ct. *Grav* 2B **22**
Echo Sq. *Grav* 2B **22**
Edam Ct. *Sidc* 3D **14**
Eden Clo. *Bex* 4C **16**
Edendale Rd. *Bexh* 1C **6**
Eden Pl. *Grav* 7A **12**
Eden Rd. *Bex* 4B **16**
Edgar Clo. *Swan* 3E **24**
Edgefield Clo. *Dart* 1C **18**
Edge Hill Ct. *Sidc* 4C **14**
Edgehill Gdns. *Ist R* 1J **29**
Edgehill Rd. *Chst* 4A **14**
Edgington Way. *Sidc* 7F **15**
Edinburgh Ct. *Eri* 7H **3**
Edinburgh M. *Til* 3A **12**
Edington Rd. *SE2* 3A **2**
Edison Gro. *SE18* 1C **4**
Edison Rd. *Well* 1C **4**
Ediva Rd. *Meop* 5K **29**
Edmund Clo. *Meop* 5K **29**
Edmund Rd. *Well* 3D **4**
Edwards Gdns. *Swan* 4C **24**
Edwards Rd. *Belv* 4E **2**
Edwin Arnold Ct. *Sidc* 4C **14**
Edwin Clo. *Bexh* 6D **2**
Edwin Petty Pl. *Dart* 7D **8**
Edwin Rd. *Dart* 3G **17**
Edwin St. *Grav* 7A **12**
Egerton Av. *Swan* 7E **16**
Egerton Clo. *Dart* 1G **17**
Eglantine La.
F'ham & Hort K 7B **26**
Eglinton Rd. *Swans* 6C **10**
Elbourne Trad. Est. *Belv* 3F **3**
Elder Clo. *Sidc* 1C **14**
Elgar Gdns. *Til* 1K **11**
Eliot Rd. *Dart* 5C **8**
Elizabeth Clo. *Til* 2A **12**
Elizabeth Ct. *Grav* 6K **11**
Elizabeth Garrett Anderson Ho.
Belv 3E **2**
(off Ambrook Rd.)
Elizabeth Huggins Cotts. *Grav* 2A **22**
Elizabeth Pl. *F'ham* 6A **26**
Elizabeth St. *Grnh* 5F **9**
Ellenborough Rd. *Sidc* 5G **15**
Ellerman Rd. *Til* 1J **11**
Ellerslie. *Grav* 7C **12**
Elliott St. *Grav* 7C **12**
Ellis Clo. *Swan* 4C **24**
Ellison Rd. *Sidc* 1A **14**
Ellis Way. *Dart* 2A **18**
Elmbourne Dri. *Belv* 4F **3**
Elm Clo. *Dart* 1H **17**
Elmcroft Av. *Sidc* 7C **4**
Elm Dri. *Swan* 2C **24**
Elmfield Clo. *Grav* 1A **22**
Elmfield Ct. *Well* 1E **4**

Elm Gro. *Eri* 7H **3**
Elmhurst. *Belv* 6C **2**
Elmhurst. *Grnh* 6J **9**
Elmington Clo. *Bex* 6A **6**
Elm Pde. *Sidc* 4D **14**
Elm Rd. *Dart* 1J **17**
Elm Rd. *Eri* 1F **7**
Elm Rd. *Grav* 3B **22**
Elm Rd. *Grnh* 6F **9**
Elm Rd. *Sidc* 4D **14**
Elmstead Rd. *Eri* 1D **6**
Elmsted Cres. *Well* 6A **2**
Elmwood Dri. *Bex* 7H **5**
Elrick Clo. *Eri* 6J **3**
Elsa Rd. *Well* 2E **4**
Elstree Gdns. *Belv* 4C **2**
Eltham Crematorium. *SE9* . . .4A **4**
Elwick Ct. *Dart* 4F **7**
Elwill Way. *Ist R* 1J **29**
Ely Clo. *Eri* 2E **6**
Embassy Ct. *Sidc* 3E **14**
Embassy Ct. *Well* 3E **4**
Emersons Av. *Swan* 7E **16**
Emerton Clo. *Bexh* 4H **5**
Emes Rd. *Eri* 7G **3**
Empress Rd. *Grav* 7D **12**
Ennerdale Rd. *Bexh* 1K **5**
Epsom Clo. *Bexh* 3A **6**
Erica Ct. *Swan* 4D **24**
Erith. 5J **3**
ERITH & DISTRICT HOSPITAL.
. . . . .6H **3**
Erith High St. *Eri* 5J **3**
Erith Mus. 5J **3**
(Library)
Erith Rd. *Belv & Eri* 5E **2**
Erith Rd. *Bexh & N Hth* 4A **6**
Erith Small Bus. Cen. Eri 6K **3**
(off Erith High St.)
Ermington Rd. *SE9* 2A **14**
Esher Clo. *Bex* 1H **15**
Eskdale Clo. *Dart* 1D **18**
Eskdale Rd. *Bexh* 2K **5**
Essenden Rd. *Belv* 5E **2**
Essex Rd. *Dart* 6J **7**
(in two parts)
Essex Rd. *Grav* 1K **21**
Essex Rd. *Long* 2A **28**
Etfield Gro. *Sidc* 5E **14**
Ethelbert Rd. *Dart* 4K **17**
Ethelbert Rd. *Eri* 7G **3**
Ethronvi Rd. *Bexh* 3H **5**
Eton Way. *Dart* 4H **7**
Europa Trad. Est. *Eri* 5H **3**
Evans Clo. *Grnh* 5H **9**
Evenden Rd. *Meop* 7K **29**
Evenlode Ho. *SE2* 2A **2**
(off Coralline Wlk.)
Everest Clo. *N'fleet* 3H **21**
Everest Pl. *Swan* 4C **24**
Everett Wlk. *Belv* 5D **2**
Everglade Clo. *Hart* 4C **28**
Eversley Av. *Bexh* 2C **6**
Eversley Cross. *Bexh* 2D **6**
Evesham Rd. *Grav* 2C **22**
Evry Rd. *Sidc* 6F **15**
Exeter Rd. *Grav* 3C **22**
Exeter Rd. *Well* 2B **4**
Exmouth Rd. *Well* 1F **5**
Eynsford Cres. *Bex* 1F **15**
Eynsford Rd. *Grnh* 5K **9**
Eynsford Rd. *Swan* 6C **24**
Eynsham Dri. *SE2* 3A **2**
Eynswood Dri. *Sidc* 5E **14**

F

Factory Rd. *N'fleet* 6F **11**
Faesten Way. *Bex* 3D **16**
Fairacre Pl. *Hart* 3B **28**
Fairby Grange. *Hart* 6B **28**
Fairby La. *Hart* 6B **28**
Fairfax Rd. *Til* 1J **11**
Fairfield Clo. *Sidc* 6C **4**
Fairfield Rd. *Bexh* 2J **5**
Fairfields. *Grav* 5D **22**

Fairford Av. *Bexh* 1C **6**
Fairlawn Av. *Bexh* 2G **5**
Fairlight Cross. *Long* 3E **28**
Fairmont Clo. *Belv* 5D **2**
Fairoak Dri. *SE9* 5A **4**
Fairseat La. *Fair* 7K **31**
Fairview. *Eri* 7K **3**
Fairview. *Fawk* 3E **30**
Fairview Gdns. *Meop* 5K **29**
Fairview Rd. *Ist R* 7G **21**
Fairwater Av. *Well* 4D **4**
Fairway. *Bexh* 5H **5**
Fairway Dri. *Dart* 7C **8**
Fairway, The. *Grav* 2K **21**
Falcon Clo. *Dart* 5A **8**
Falcon M. *Grav* 1H **21**
Falconwood. 4C **4**
Falconwood. (Junct.) 4A **4**
Falconwood Av. *Well* 2A **4**
Falconwood Pde. *Well* 4B **4**
Fallowfield. *Bean* 3J **19**
Falstaff Clo. *Dart* 7D **6**
Faraday Av. *Sidc* 2D **14**
Faraday Rd. *Well* 3D **4**
Farley Rd. *Grav* 1E **22**
Farlow Clo. *N'fleet* 3J **21**
Farm Av. *Swan* 3B **24**
Farmcroft. *Grav* 2K **21**
Farm Holt. *New Ash* 1J **31**
Farm Pl. *Dart* 4F **7**
Farm Va. *Bex* 6A **6**
Farnham Rd. *Well* 2F **5**
Farningham. 7A **26**
Farningham Hill Rd.
F'ham 5H **25**
Farnol Rd. *Dart* 5B **8**
Farriers Clo. *Grav* 1E **22**
Farrington Pl. *Chst* 7A **14**
Farthing Clo. *Dart* 4A **8**
Farwell Rd. *Sidc* 4E **14**
Fawkes Av. *Dart* 2A **18**
Fawkham. 7J **27**
Fawkham Av. *Long* 3F **29**
Fawkham Green. 2E **30**
Fawkham Grn. Rd. *Fawk* 3E **30**
FAWKHAM MANOR BMI
HOSPITAL. 1F **31**
Fawkham Rd. *Fawk* 4C **30**
Fawkham Rd. *Hart* 4A **28**
Faygate Cres. *Bexh* 5K **5**
Federation Rd. *SE2* 4A **2**
Feenan Highway. *Til* 1A **12**
Felix Mnr. *Chst* 6B **14**
Felixstowe Rd. *SE2* 3A **2**
Felton Lea. *Sidc* 5C **14**
Fendyke Rd. *Belv* 4B **2**
Fen Gro. *Sidc* 5C **4**
Fens Way. *Swan* 6F **17**
Fenswood Clo. *Bex* 6K **5**
Ferby Ct. *SE9* 3A **14**
(off Main Rd.)
Ferguson Av. *Grav* 4B **22**
Fernbrook Av. *Sidc* 5B **4**
Fern Clo. *Eri* 1G **7**
Fern Ct. *Bexh* 4K **5**
Ferndale Clo. *Bexh* 1H **5**
Ferndale Rd. *Grav* 2A **22**
Ferndell Av. *Bex* 3C **16**
Ferndene. *Long* 3G **29**
Fernheath Way. *Dart* 5C **16**
Ferry Rd. *Til* 3K **11**
Festival Av. *Long* 3G **29**
Festival Clo. *Bex* 1G **15**
Festival Clo. *Eri* 7K **3**
Fiddler's Clo. *Grnh* 4J **9**
Fielding Av. *Til* 1A **12**
Filborough Way. *Grav* 2G **23**
Filston Rd. *Eri* 5G **3**
Finch Ct. *Sidc* 3E **14**
Finchley Clo. *Dart* 6B **8**
Finsbury Way. *Bex* 6J **5**
Firecrest Clo. *Long* 3E **28**
Firmin Rd. *Dart* 5H **7**
Firside Gro. *Sidc* 1C **14**
First Av. *Bexh* 7A **2**
First Av. *N'fleet* 1H **21**
Firs, The. *Bex* 1C **16**

Firs, The. *Sidc* 3C **14**
Fishermens Hill. *N'fleet* 5E **10**
Fishers Way. *Belv* 1G **3**
Fitzroy Ct. *Dart* 1C **18**
   (off Churchill Clo.)
Fiveash Rd. *Grav* 7J **11**
Five Wents. *Swan* 2F **25**
Flats, The. *Grnh* 5K **9**
Flaxman Ct. *Belv* 5E **2**
   (off Hoddesdon Rd.)
Flaxton Rd. *SE18* 1A **4**
Fleet Av. *Dart* 1D **18**
Fleetdale Pde. *Dart* 1D **18**
Fleet Downs. 1D **18**
Fleet Houses. *S'fleet* 6E **20**
Fleet Rd. *Dart* 1C **18**
Fleet Rd. *N'fleet* 3F **21**
Fleming Gdns. *Til* 1B **12**
Flora St. *Belv* 5D **2**
Florence Farm Mobile Home Pk.
   W King 6A **30**
Florence Rd. *SE2* 4A **2**
Flowerhill Way. *Ist R* 7H **21**
Foley Ct. *Dart* 1C **18**
   (off Churchill Clo.)
Foord Clo. *Dart* 2F **19**
Foots Cray. 6F **15**
Foots Cray High St. *Sidc* 6F **15**
Foots Cray La. *Sidc* 1F **15**
Footscray Rd. *SE9* 2A **14**
Ford Rd. *N'fleet* 5E **10**
Forest Rd. *Eri* 1F **7**
Forest Way. *Sidc* 7A **4**
Forge La. *Grav* 2E **22**
Forge La. *Hort K* 4D **26**
Forge La. *Shorne* 5K **23**
Forresters Cres. *Bexh* 4A **6**
Fortress Distribution Pk.
   Til 4K **11**
Fort Rd. *Til* 4A **12**
Fortrye Clo. *N'fleet* 2H **21**
Fortuna Clo. *Hart* 4C **28**
Forty Foot Way. *SE9* 7A **4**
Fosset Lodge. *Bexh* 1B **6**
Fossington Rd. *Belv* 4B **2**
Fountain Ct. *Sidc* 6E **4**
Fountain Wlk. *N'fleet* 6H **11**
Fourth Av. *N'fleet* 1H **21**
Fowlers Clo. *Sidc* 5H **15**
Foxberry Wlk. *N'fleet* 3G **21**
   (off Ashmore Gdns.)
Foxbury. *New Ash* 3H **31**
Foxbury Av. *Chst* 6A **14**
Fox Hollow Dri. *Bexh* 3G **5**
Foxhounds La. *S'fleet* 3D **20**
Fox Ho. Rd. *Belv* 5F **3**
   (in two parts)
Foxwood Gro. *N'fleet* 1H **21**
Foxwood Rd. *Bean* 3J **19**
Foxwood Way. *Long* 2G **29**
Francis Av. *Bexh* 2K **5**
Francis Rd. *Dart* 5J **7**
Franklin Rd. *Bexh* 1H **5**
Franklin Rd. *Grav* 5C **22**
Franks La. *Hort K* 5C **26**
Fraser Clo. *Bex* 1B **16**
Fraser Rd. *Eri* 5G **3**
Freeland Ct. *Sidc* 3D **14**
Freeland Way. *Eri* 1F **7**
Freeman Rd. *Grav* 3D **22**
Fremantle Ho. *Til* 1J **11**
Fremantle Rd. *Belv* 4E **2**
Frensham Rd. *SE9* 2A **14**
Freta Rd. *Bexh* 5J **5**
Friars Wlk. *SE2* 5B **2**
Friday Rd. *Eri* 5H **3**
Frimley Ct. *Sidc* 5F **15**
Frinsted Rd. *Eri* 7H **3**
Frinton Rd. *Sidc* 2H **15**
Friswell Pl. *Bexh* 4K **5**
Frobisher Rd. *Eri* 7K **3**
Frobisher Way. *Grav* 5D **22**
Frobisher Way. *Grnh* 4J **9**
Frognal Av. *Sidc* 6D **14**
Frognal Corner. (Junct.) . . .6C **14**
Frognal Pl. *Sidc* 6D **14**
Fuchsia St. *SE2* 5A **2**

Fulwich Rd. *Dart* 6A **8**
Furner Clo. *Dart* 3E **6**

G

Gable Clo. *Dart* 5F **7**
Gables, The. *Long* 2F **29**
Gabriel Gdns. *Grav* 5D **22**
Gabrielspring Rd. *Fawk* 2A **30**
Gabrielspring Rd. E.
   Fawk 2B **30**
Gainsborough Av. *Dart* 5H **7**
Gainsborough Av. *Til* 1K **11**
Gainsborough Dri. *N'fleet* . . .3G **21**
Gainsborough Sq. *Bexh* 3G **5**
Galleon Boulevd. *Dart* 4E **8**
Galleon Clo. *Eri* 4H **3**
Galley Hill Ind. Est. *Swans* . . .5B **10**
Galley Hill Rd. *Swans* 5C **10**
Galloway Dri. Rd. *Dart* 7D **6**
Gallows Wood. *Fawk* 4D **30**
Galsworthy Rd. *Til* 1B **12**
Galpp Clo. *W King* 7B **30**
Garden Av. *Bexh* 3K **5**
Garden Pl. *Dart* 3J **17**
Garden Row. *N'fleet* 3J **21**
Gargery Clo. *Grav* 1F **23**
Garland Rd. *SE18* 1A **4**
Garleon Clo. *Eri* 4H **3**
Garrard Clo. *Bexh* 3K **5**
Garrick St. *Grav* 6A **12**
Garrolds Clo. *Swan* 2C **24**
Garrow. *Long* 3E **28**
Gascoyne Dri. *Dart* 3E **6**
Gasson Rd. *Swans* 6B **10**
Gateacre Ct. *Sidc* 4E **14**
Gateway Pde. *Grav* 4E **22**
Gattons Way. *Sidc* 4J **15**
Gatwick Rd. *Grav* 3A **22**
Gaylor Rd. *Til* 1J **11**
Gayton Rd. *SE2* 3A **2**
Gazelle Glade. *Grav* 5E **22**
Geddes Pl. *Bexh* 4K **5**
   (off Arnsberga Way)
Genesta Glade. *Grav* 5F **23**
Gerald Rd. *Grav* 7D **12**
Gerda Rd. *SE9* 2A **14**
Gerdview Dri. *Dart* 4H **17**
Gertrude Rd. *Belv* 4E **2**
Gibson Clo. *N'fleet* 3J **21**
Gideon Clo. *Belv* 4F **3**
Gilbert Clo. *Swans* 6A **10**
Gilbert Rd. *Belv* 3E **2**
Gildenhill Rd. *Swan* 7H **17**
Gill Cres. *N'fleet* 3J **21**
Gillies Rd. *W King* 5B **30**
Gills Rd. *S Dar* 1F **27**
Gipsy Rd. *Well* 7B **2**
Glades, The. *Grav* 6C **22**
Gladeswood Rd. *Belv* 4F **3**
Gladstone Rd. *Dart* 6A **8**
Glebelands. *Dart* 4E **6**
Glebe Pl. *Hort K* 4D **26**
Glebe Rd. *Grav* 1J **21**
Glebe Way. *Eri* 6J **3**
Glen Ct. *Sidc* 4D **14**
Glendale. *Swan* 5E **24**
Glendale Rd. *Eri* 4G **3**
Glendale Rd. *N'fleet* 4H **21**
Glendale Way. *SE28* 1A **2**
Glengall Rd. *Bexh* 3H **5**
Glenhurst Av. *Bex* 1J **15**
Glenmore Rd. *Well* 1C **4**
Glenrosa Gdns. *Grav* 5E **22**
Glenrose Ct. *Sidc* 5E **14**
Glenview. *SE2* 6B **2**
Glen Vw. *Grav* 1B **22**
Glenwood Ct. *Sidc* 4D **14**
Glimpsing Grn. *Eri* 3C **2**
Gloucester Av. *Sidc* 2B **14**
Gloucester Av. *Well* 4C **4**
Gloucester Ct. *Til* 2J **11**
Gloucester Pde. *Sidc* 5D **4**
Gloucester Rd. *Belv* 5D **2**
Gloucester Rd. *Dart* 7G **7**
Gloucester Rd. *Grav* 4B **22**
Glover Clo. *SE2* 4A **2**

Gloxinia Rd. *S'fleet* 6E **20**
Glynde Rd. *Bexh* 3G **5**
Glyn Dri. *Sidc* 4E **14**
Godstow Rd. *SE2* 2A **2**
Goldsel Rd. *Swan* 5C **24**
Golf Links Av. *Grav* 5A **22**
Goodwin Dri. *Sidc* 3G **15**
Goodwood Cres. *Grav* 5B **22**
Gordon Clo. *E Til* 1J **13**
Gordon Pl. *Grav* 6B **12**
Gordon Promenade. *Grav* 6B **12**
Gordon Promenade E.
   Grav 6B **12**
Gordon Rd. *Belv* 4G **3**
Gordon Rd. *Dart* 7J **7**
Gordon Rd. *N'fleet* 7H **11**
Gordon Rd. *Sidc* 5B **4**
Gore Cotts. *Grn St* 3D **18**
Gore Rd. *Dart* 3D **18**
Gorringe Av. *S Dar* 2E **26**
Gorse Hill. *F'ham* . . . . .7B **26** & 2A **30**
Gorse Way. *Hart* 5C **28**
Gorsewood Rd.
   Hart & Long 5C **28**
   (in two parts)
Goss Hill. *Swan* 6H **17**
Gothic Clo. *Dart* 3J **17**
Gouge Av. *N'fleet* 1H **21**
Grace Av. *Bexh* 2J **5**
Graham Rd. *Bexh* 4K **5**
Graham Ter. *Sidc* 6E **4**
   (off Westerham Dri.)
Granby Rd. *Grav* 6F **11**
   (in two parts)
Grange Clo. *Sidc* 3D **14**
Grange Cres. *Dart* 6C **8**
Grange Ho. *Eri* 2F **7**
Grange Ho. *Grav* 7K **11**
Grange La. *Hart* 7D **28**
Grange Rd. *Grav* 7K **11**
Grange, The. *S Dar* 1E **26**
Grange, The. *W King* 7C **30**
Grange Way. *Eri* 2K **3**
Grange Way. *Hart* 6C **28**
Grangeways Clo. *N'fleet* 4J **21**
Grangewood. *Bex* 1J **15**
Granton Rd. *Sidc* 6F **15**
Granville M. *Sidc* 4D **14**
Granville Rd. *Grav* 7J **11**
Granville Rd. *Sidc* 4D **14**
Granville Rd. *Well* 3F **5**
Grasmere Rd. *Bexh* 2B **6**
Grassington Rd. *Sidc* 4D **14**
Grass Rd. *Long* 5F **29**
Gravel Hill. *Bexh* 5A **6**
Gravel Hill Clo. *Bexh* 5A **6**
Gravel Pit La. *SE9* 5A **4**
Gravel Rd. *S at H* 7C **18**
Gravesend. 6A **12**
Gravesend & Northfleet F.C.
   . . . . .5D **10**
GRAVESEND & NORTH KENT
   HOSPITAL. 6K **11**
Gravesend Rd.
   Shorne & High 3J **23**
Gravesham Ct. *Grav* 7A **12**
Gravesham Mus. 6A **12**
Grays Farm Rd. *Orp* 7E **14**
Grazeley Clo. *Bexh* 5B **6**
Gt. Queen St. *Dart* 7A **8**
Greenacre. *Dart* 2J **17**
Greenacre Clo. *Swan* 4D **24**
Greenacres. *Sidc* 4D **14**
Greenbanks. *Dart* 2K **17**
Green Ct. Rd. *Swan* 6C **24**
Greendale Wlk. *N'fleet* 4H **21**
Green Farm La. *Shorne* 2K **23**
Greenfield Rd. *Dart* 5C **16**
Greenfinches. *Long* 3E **28**
Greenhill Rd. *N'fleet* 2J **21**
Greenhithe. 4J **9**
Greenhithe Clo. *Sidc* 7B **4**
Greening St. *SE2* 4A **2**
Green La. *Meop* 7K **29**
Green La. *Shorne* 6J **23**
Grn. Manor Way. *Grav* 4C **10**
Greenmead. *Eri* 3C **2**

Green Pl. *Dart* 5D **6**
Greenside. *Bex* 1H **15**
Greenside. *Swan* 2C **24**
Green Street Green. 6H **19**
Green St. Grn. Rd. *Dart* 1C **18**
   (in three parts)
Green, The. *Bexh* 1K **5**
Green, The. *Dart* 2E **18**
Green, The. *Orp* 7E **14**
Green, The. *Sidc* 4D **14**
Green, The. *Well* 4B **4**
Green Va. *Bexh* 5G **5**
Green Wlk. *Dart* 5E **6**
Green Way. *Hart* 5B **28**
Greenways. *Long* 3G **29**
GREENWICH & BEXLEY COTTAGE
   HOSPICE. 5A **2**
Greenwood Clo. *Sidc* 2D **14**
Greenwood Rd. *Bex* 4C **16**
Gresham Av. *Hart* 5C **28**
Gresham Clo. *Bex* 6H **5**
Gresswell Clo. *Sidc* 3D **14**
Greyhound Commercial Cen., The.
   Dart 5D **6**
Greyhound Way. *Dart* 5D **6**
Grieves Rd. *N'fleet* 3J **21**
Griffin Wlk. *Grnh* 5G **9**
Groombridge Clo. *Well* 5D **4**
Grosvenor Cres. *Dart* 5J **7**
Grosvenor Rd. *Belv* 6E **2**
Grosvenor Rd. *Bexh* 5G **5**
Grosvenor Sq. *Long* 3B **28**
Grovebury Clo. *Eri* 6H **3**
Grovebury Ct. *Bexh* 5A **6**
Grovebury Rd. *SE2* 2A **2**
Groveherst Rd. *Dart* 3A **8**
Grovelands Rd. *Orp* 7D **14**
Grove Rd. *Belv* 6D **2**
Grove Rd. *Bexh* 4B **6**
Grove Rd. *N'fleet* 5E **10**
Grove, The. *Bexh* 4G **5**
Grove, The. *Grav* 7A **12**
Grove, The. *Sidc* 4H **15**
Grove, The. *Swan* 3E **24**
Grove, The. *Swans* 5C **10**
Grubb Street. 1J **27**
Guild Rd. *Eri* 7K **3**
Gulliver Rd. *Sidc* 2A **14**
Gunfleet Clo. *Grav* 7D **12**
Gunn Rd. *Swans* 6B **10**
Gwillim Clo. *Sidc* 5D **4**
Gwynn Rd. *N'fleet* 2F **21**

H

Haddon Gro. *Sidc* 7C **4**
Hadley Rd. *Belv* 4D **2**
Hadlow Rd. *Sidc* 4D **14**
Hadlow Rd. *Well* 7A **2**
Hadlow Way. *Ist R* 7H **21**
Haig Gdns. *Grav* 7B **12**
Hailey Rd. *Eri* 2E **2**
Halcot Av. *Bexh* 5A **6**
Haldane Gdns. *Grav* 1F **21**
Haldane Rd. *SE28* 1B **2**
Halfway St. *Sidc* 7A **4**
Halifield Dri. *Belv* 3C **2**
Hallford Way. *Dart* 6H **7**
Hall Place. 6B **6**
Hall Pl. Cres. *Bex* 5B **6**
Hall Place Mus. 6B **6**
Hall Rd. *Dart* 4A **8**
Hall Rd. *N'fleet* 3F **21**
Halstead Rd. *Eri* 1D **6**
Halt Robin La. *Belv* 4F **3**
Halt Robin Rd. *Belv* 4E **2**
   (in two parts)
Hambledown Rd. *Sidc* 7A **4**
Hamerton Rd. *N'fleet* 5E **10**
Hamilton Ct. *Eri* 7K **3**
   (off Frobisher Rd.)
Hamilton Rd. *Bexh* 2H **5**
Hamilton Rd. *Sidc* 4D **14**
Hamilton Wlk. *Eri* 7K **3**
Hamlet Ho. *Eri* 7J **3**
Hampton Cres. *Grav* 2D **22**

Hampton Ho.—Hythe St. (Lwr.)

Hampton Ho. Bexh 2A 6
(off Erith Rd.)
Hamshades Clo. Sidc 3C 14
Hanbury Wlk. Bex 3D 16
Hanover Pl. New Ash 2J 31
Hanover Way. Bexh 3G 5
Hansol Rd. Bexh 5H 5
Harbex Clo. Bex 7A 6
Harborough Av. Sidc 7B 4
Harcourt Av. Sidc 6F 5
Harcourt Rd. Bexh 4H 5
Harden Rd. N'fleet 3J 21
Harding Rd. Bexh 2J 5
Hardwick Ct. Eri 6H 3
Hardwick Cres. Dart 6C 8
Hardy Av. N'fleet 2H 21
Hardy Ct. Eri 7K 3
Hardy Gro. Dart 4B 8
Harefield Rd. Sidc 3G 15
Harfst Way. Swan 1B 24
Harland Av. Sidc 3A 14
Harlequin Ho. Eri 3C 2
(off Kale Rd.)
Harlington Rd. Bexh 3H 5
Harman Av. Grav 5A 22
Harman Dri. Sidc 6C 4
Harmer Rd. Swans 6C 10
Harmer St. Grav 6B 12
Harnetts Clo. Swan 7C 24
Harold Av. Belv 5D 2
Harold Rd. Dart 4A 18
Harold Wilson Ho. SE28 1A 2
Harris Clo. N'fleet 3J 21
Harris Rd. Bexh 1H 5
Harrowby Gdns. N'fleet 2H 21
Harrow Mnr. Way. SE2 1A 2
Hart Dyke Cres. Swan 3C 24
Hart Dyke Rd. Swan 2C 24
Hartfield Pl. N'fleet 7G 11
Hartford Rd. Bex 6K 5
Hartlands Clo. Bex 6J 5
Hartley. 4C 28
Hartley Bottom Rd.
Hart & Long 7E 28
Hartley Bottom Rd.
Sev & New Ash 6K 31
Hartley Green. 5B 28
Hartley Hill. 1K 31
Hartley Hill. Hart 1K 31
Hartley Rd. Long 2B 28
Hartley Rd. Well 7A 2
Hart Shaw. Long 2E 28
Hartshill Rd. N'fleet 2J 21
Hartslock Dri. SE2 2B 2
Harvel Cres. SE2 5B 2
Harvest Way. Swan 7C 24
Harvill Rd. Sidc 5H 15
Haslemere Rd. Bexh 2J 5
Hasted Clo. Grnh 6K 9
Hatherley Cres. Sidc 2D 14
Hatherley Rd. Sidc 4D 14
Hattersfield Clo. Belv 4D 2
Hatton Clo. N'fleet 3H 21
Havelock Rd. Belv 4D 2
Havelock Rd. Dart 7G 7
Havelock Rd. Grav 1J 21
Haven Clo. Ist R 1J 29
Haven Clo. Sidc 6F 15
Haven Clo. Swan 2E 24
Havengore Av. Grav 7D 12
Haven Hill. Hods 6K 31
Havisham Rd. Grav 2F 23
Hawkins Av. Grav 4B 22
Hawley. 4A 18
Hawley Rd.
Dart & S at H 2K 17
Hawley Ter. Dart 4B 18
Hawley Va. Dart 5B 18
(in two parts)
Hawthorn Clo. Grav 4A 22
Hawthorn Cotts. Well 3D 4
(off Hook La.)
Hawthorn Pl. Eri 5G 3
Hawthorn Rd. Bexh 4J 5
Hawthorn Rd. Dart 2J 17
Hawthorns. Hart 4C 28
Hawthorn Ter. Sidc 5C 4
Hayes Rd. Grnh 7F 9
Hayes Ter. Shorne 5K 23
Haynes Rd. N'fleet 3J 21
Hayward Clo. Dart 5C 6
Hayward Dri. Dart 2A 18
Hazeldene Rd. Well 2F 5
Hazel Dri. Eri 1F 7
Hazel End. Swan 5D 24
Hazel Rd. Dart 2J 17
Hazel Rd. Eri 1F 7
Heath Av. Bexh 6B 2
Heathclose. Swan 2D 24
Heathclose Av. Dart 7G 7
Heathclose Rd. Dart 1F 17
Heathdene Dri. Belv 4F 3
Heath End Rd. Bex 1D 16
Heatherbank Clo. Dart 6D 6
Heather Ct. Sidc 6G 15
Heather Dri. Dart 7F 7
Heather End. Swan 4C 24
Heatherside Rd. Sidc 3F 15
Heathfield. Chst 6A 14
Heathfield Pde. Swan 2B 24
Heathfield Rd. Bexh 4J 5
Heath Gdns. Dart 1H 17
Heath Ho. Sidc 4C 14
Heathlands Ri. Dart 6G 7
Heath La. (Lower). Dart 1H 17
Heath La. (Upper). Dart 2F 17
Heathlee Rd. Dart 6D 6
Heath Rd. Bex 1B 16
Heath Rd. Dart 6E 6
Heath Side. 2E 16
Heathside Av. Bexh 1H 5
Heath St. Dart 7J 7
Heathview Av. Dart 6D 6
Heathview Cres. Dart 1F 17
Heathview Dri. SE2 6B 2
HEATHVIEW DAY CENTRE. 6A 2
Heath Way. Eri 1B 6
Heathwood Gdns. Swan 2B 24
Heathwood Wlk. Bex 1D 16
Hedge Pl. Rd. Grnh 6G 9
Hedgerows, The. N'fleet 2H 21
Helen Clo. Dart 7G 7
Hemmings Clo. Sidc 2E 14
Hemsted Rd. Eri 7J 3
Henderson Dri. Dart 4A 8
Henfield Clo. Bex 6K 5
Hengist Rd. Eri 7F 3
Hengrove Ct. Bex 1H 15
Henhurst Rd. Cobh 7D 22
Henley Deane. N'fleet 4H 21
Herald Wlk. Dart 5A 8
Herbert Rd. Bexh 2H 5
Herbert Rd. Swan 6G 17
Herbert Rd. Swans 6C 10
Hereward Lincoln Ho.
N'fleet 6G 11
(off London Rd.)
Heritage Quay. Grav 6B 12
Heron Cres. Sidc 3B 14
Herongate Rd. Swan 6D 16
Heron Hill. Belv 5D 2
Heron Ho. Sidc 3E 14
Hertford Wlk. Belv 5E 2
Hesketh Av. Dart 1C 18
Hever Av. W King 7B 30
Hever Ct. Rd. Grav 6B 22
Hever Rd. W King 6B 30
Heversham Rd. Bexh 2K 5
Hever Wood Rd. W King 7B 30
Hewett Pl. Swan 4C 24
Hextable. 7E 16
Hibbs Clo. Swan 2C 24
Hibernia Dri. Grav 3E 22
Hibernia Point. SE2 2B 2
(off Wolvercote Rd.)
Highbanks Clo. Well 1E 4
High Beeches. Sidc 5H 15
High Cft. Cotts. Swan 4F 25
Highcross Rd. S'fleet 5A 20
Highfield Av. Eri 6F 3
Highfield Cotts. Dart 6G 17
Highfield Rd. Bexh 5J 5
Highfield Rd. Dart 7J 7
Highfield Rd. N. Dart 6J 7
Highfield Rd. S. Dart 7J 7
High Firs. Swan 4D 24
High Gro. SE18 1A 4
Highland Rd. Bexh 5K 5
Highlands Farm Bus. Pk.
Swan 1F 25
Highlands Hill. Swan 1F 25
Highmead. SE18 1C 4
High Rd. Dart 3H 17
Highstead Cres. Eri 1D 6
High St. Bean 3J 19
High St. Dart 6K 7
High St. F'ham 6K 25
High St. Grav 6A 12
High St. Grnh 4J 9
High St. N'fleet 6E 10
High St. Swan 3E 24
High St. Swans 5C 10
High Trees. Dart 6C 8
High Vw. Rd. Sidc 4E 14
Hilary Clo. Eri 1A 6
Hilda May Av. Swan 3D 24
Hilden Dri. Eri 2K 3
Hillary Av. N'fleet 3H 21
Hill Brow. Dart 6E 6
Hill Brow Clo. Bex 4C 16
Hill Clo. Ist R 7H 21
Hill Cres. Bex 1B 16
Hillcrest. Sidc 7D 4
Hillcrest Dri. Grnh 5H 9
Hillcrest Rd. Dart 7D 6
Hill Ho. Rd. Dart 7D 8
Hillingdon Rd. Bexh 2B 6
Hillingdon Rd. Grav 2A 22
Hill Ri. Dart 5E 18
Hill Rd. Dart 2K 17
Hillsgrove Clo. Well 7A 2
Hillside. 4G 3
Hillside. Dart 5F 19
Hillside. Eri 4G 3
Hillside. F'ham 7A 26
Hillside Av. Grav 2C 22
Hillside Ct. Swan 4F 25
Hillside Dri. Grav 2C 22
Hillside Rd. Dart 6F 7
Hill, The. N'fleet 6F 11
Hilltop Gdns. Dart 5A 8
Hill Vw. Dri. Well 2B 4
Hillview Ho. Grav 1B 22
Hill Vw. Rd. Long 3E 28
Hind Cres. Eri 6H 3
Hinksey Path. SE2 2B 2
Hive La. N'fleet 6E 10
(in two parts)
Hive, The. N'fleet 6E 10
Hobart Rd. Til 1K 11
Hoblands End. Chst 6B 14
Hockenden. 2A 24
Hockenden La. Swan 3A 24
Hoddesdon Rd. Belv 5E 2
Hogs La. Grav 3G 21
Hogs Orchard. Swan 1G 25
Holbeach Gdns. Sidc 6B 4
Holbrook Ho. Chst 7A 14
Holbrook La. Chst 7A 14
Holcote Clo. Belv 3C 2
Hollands Clo. Shorne 5K 23
(in two parts)
Hollies Av. Sidc 2C 14
Hollies, The. Grav 6C 22
Hollies, The. Long 3F 29
Hollingbourne Av. Bexh 1J 5
Hollybrake Clo. Chst 7A 14
Hollybush Rd. Grav 2B 22
Holly Ct. Sidc 4E 14
(off Sidcup Hill)
Holly Gdns. Bexh 4B 6
Holly Hill Rd. Belv 5F 3
Holly Rd. Dart 1J 17
Hollytree Av. Swan 2D 24
Hollytree Pde. Sidc 6F 15
(off Sidcup Hill)
Hollywood Way. Eri 2K 3
Holmbury Mnr. Sidc 4D 14
Holmesdale Hill. S Dar 1D 26
Holmesdale Rd. Bexh 2G 5
Holmesdale Rd. S Dar 1D 26
Holmhurst Rd. Belv 5F 3
Holmleigh Av. Dart 5H 7
Holmsdale Gro. Bexh 2D 6
Holstein Way. Eri 3B 2
Holyoake Mt. Grav 1C 22
Homefield Clo. Swan 3E 24
Homefield Rd. S at H 1B 26
Home Gdns. Dart 6K 7
Home Hill. Swan 7E 16
Homemead. Grav 7A 12
Homemead. Grnh 6J 9
Home Mead Clo. Grav 7A 12
Home Orchard. Dart 6K 7
(in two parts)
Homer Clo. Bexh 1B 6
Homestead, The. Dart 5D 6
(off Crayford High St.)
Homestead, The. Dart 6H 7
(West Hill Dri.)
Homewood Cres. Chst 6B 14
Honeyden Rd. Sidc 6H 15
Honeyfield. Swan 6E 16
Honiton Rd. Well 2C 4
Hookfields. N'fleet 3H 21
Hook Green. 4F 17
(Dartford)
Hook Green. 6K 29
(Meopham)
Hook Green. 6D 20
(Southfleet)
Hook Grn. La. Dart 3E 16
Hook Grn. Rd. S'fleet 7B 20
Hook La. Well 5C 4
Hope Rd. Swans 6C 10
Hopewell Dri. Grav 5E 22
Horizon Ho. Swan 4D 24
Horley Clo. Bexh 5K 5
Hornbeam La. Bexh 2B 6
Horns Cross. 6F 9
Horn Yd. Grav 6A 12
(off Bank St.)
Horsa Rd. Eri 7F 3
Horsfield Clo. Dart 7D 8
Horsham Rd. Bexh 5K 5
Horton Kirby. 4D 26
Horton Kirby Trad. Est.
S Dar 1D 26
Horton Rd.
Hort K & S Dar 4D 26
Horton Way. F'ham 7A 26
Hoselands Vw. Hart 4B 28
Hotham Clo. S at H 7C 18
Hotham Clo. Swan 1G 25
Hottsfield. Hart 3B 28
Howard Av. Bex 1F 15
Howard Rd. Dart 6B 8
Howbury La. Eri 2F 7
Howden Clo. SE28 1B 2
Howells Clo. W King 6B 30
Hudson Rd. Bexh 2J 5
Hulsewood Clo. Dart 3G 17
Humber Rd. Dart 5J 7
Hume Av. Til 3K 11
Hume Clo. Til 3K 11
Hunters Clo. Bex 3D 16
Huntingfield Rd. Meop 7K 29
Huntley Av. N'fleet 6E 10
Hunt Rd. N'fleet 3H 21
Hurlfield. Dart 3H 17
Hurlingham Rd. Bexh 7D 2
Hurst Ct. Sidc 2D 14
Hurst La. SE2 5B 2
Hurst La. Est. SE2 5B 2
Hurst Pl. Dart 6H 7
Hurst Rd. Eri 1B 6
Hurst Rd. Sidc & Bex 2D 14
Hurst Springs. Bex 1H 15
Hurstwood Av. Bex 1H 15
Hurstwood Av. Eri 1D 6
Huxley Rd. Well 3C 4
Hyde Rd. Bexh 2J 5
Hyndford Cres. Grnh 5K 9
Hythe Av. Bexh 7C 2
Hythe St. Dart 6K 7
(in two parts)
Hythe St. (Lwr.) Dart 5K 7

A-Z Dartford & Gravesend 39

Idleigh Ct. Rd.—Lingfield Av.

I

Idleigh Ct. Rd. *Meop* 2K 31
Ifield. **7B 22**
Ifield Way. *Grav* 6C 22
Ightham Rd. *Eri* 7E 2
Imperial Bus. Est. *Grav* 6J 11
Imperial Dri. *Grav* 5E 22
Imperial Retail Pk. *Grav* 6K 11
Imperial Way. *Chst* 3A 14
Ingess Pk. *Grnh* 5K 9
Inglenorth Ct. *Swan* 6B 24
Ingleton Av. *Well* 5D 4
Inglewood. *Swan* 2D 24
Inglewood Rd. *Bexh* 4C 6
Ingoldsby Rd. *Grav* 1D 22
Ingram Rd. *Dart* 1K 17
Ingress Gdns. *Grnh* 5A 10
Ingress Park. **4K 9**
Ingress Ter. *S'fleet* 4B 20
Instone Rd. *Dart* 7J 7
Invicta Pde. *Sidc* 4E 14
Invicta Rd. *Dart* 6C 8
Ionia Wlk. *Grav* 3E 22
Iris Av. *Bex* 6H 5
Iris Cres. *Bexh* 6D 2
Iron Mill La. *Dart* 4D 6
Iron Mill Pl. *Dart* 4E 6
Irving Wlk. *Swans* 7B 10
Irving Way. *Swan* 2C 24
Istead Rise. **1J 29**
Istead Ri. *Grav* 7J 21
Ivedon Rd. *Well* 2F 5
Iverhurst Clo. *Bexh* 5G 5
Ivy Bower Clo. *Grnh* 5J 9
Ivy Clo. *Dart* 6B 8
Ivy Clo. *Grav* 4B 22
Ivy Vs. *Grnh* 5H 9
Izane Rd. *Bexh* 4J 5

J

Jackson Clo. *Grnh* 5G 9
Jacob Ho. *Eri* 2B 2
Jacobs La. *Hort K* 3D 26
Jagger Clo. *Dart* 7D 8
James Av. W King *7B 30*
(off London Rd.)
James Rd. *Dart* 7F 7
James Watt Way. *Eri* 6K 3
Jane Seymour Ct. *SE9* 7A 4
Jellicoe Av. *Grav* 3B 22
Jellicoe Av. W. *Grav* 3B 22
Jenningtree Rd. *Eri* 2K 3
Jenningtree Way. *Belv* 2G 3
Jenton Av. *Bexh* 1H 5
Jessamine Pl. *Dart* 7D 8
Jessett Clo. *Eri* 4H 3
John Newton Ct. *Well* 3E 4
John's Hole. **7E 8**
Johnson Clo. *N'fleet* 3G 21
Johnson's Way. *Grnh* 6K 9
John's Rd. *Meop* 5J 29
Joyce Green. **4A 8**
Joyce Grn. La. *Dart* 4A 8
Joyce Grn. Wlk. *Dart* 4A 8
Joydens Wood. **4C 16**
Joydens Wood Rd. *Bex* 4C 16
Joy Rd. *Grav* 1B 22
Jubilee Clo. *Grnh* 6K 9
Jubilee Ct. Dart *7J 7*
(off Spring Va. S.)
Jubilee Cres. *Grav* 2D 22
Jubilee Way. *Sidc* 2D 14
Judeth Gdns. *Grav* 5D 22
Junction Rd. *Dart* 6J 7
Juniper Wlk. *Swan* 2C 24
Jury St. *Grav* 6A 12

K

Kale Rd. *Eri* 2C 2
Kaysland Cvn Pk. *W King* 7B 30
Kay St. *Well* 1E 4
Keary Rd. *Swans* 7B 10
Keats Gdns. *Til* 2A 12
Keats Ho. *Cray* 5D 6
Keats Rd. *Belv* 3G 3
Keats Rd. *Well* 1B 4
Keightley Dri. *SE9* 1A 14
Keith Av. *S at H* 6C 18
Kelso Dri. *Grav* 4E 22
Kelvin Rd. *Til* 2K 11
Kelvin Rd. *Well* 3D 4
Kemnal Rd. *Chst* 4A 14
(in two parts)
Kempthorne St. *Grav* 6A 12
Kempton Clo. *Eri* 6G 3
Kemsing Clo. *Bex* 7H 5
Kemsley Clo. *Grnh* 6J 9
Kemsley Clo. *N'fleet* 4J 21
Kencot Way. *Eri* 2D 2
Kendall Ct. *Sidc* 3D 14
Kenia Wlk. *Grav* 3E 22
Kenilworth Ct. Dart *6C 8*
(off Bow Arrow La.)
Kenley Clo. *Bex* 7K 5
Kenmere Rd. *Well* 2F 5
Kennedy Ho. *Grav* 3H 21
Kennet Rd. *Dart* 3F 7
Kennett Ct. Swan *3D 24*
(off Oakleigh Clo.)
Kent Av. *Well* 5C 4
Kent Clo. *W King* 7B 30
Kentish Rd. *Belv* 4E 2
Kent Kraft Ind. Est. *N'fleet* 5C 10
Kent Rd. *Dart* 6J 7
Kent Rd. *Grav* 1K 21
Kent Rd. *Long* 2A 28
Kenwood Av. *Long* 3F 29
Kenwyn Rd. *Dart* 5J 7
Kestlake Rd. *Bex* 6F 5
Keston Clo. *Well* 7A 2
Keston Ct. *Bex* 7J 5
Keswick Rd. *Bexh* 1K 5
Kettlewell Ct. *Swan* 2E 24
Keyes Rd. *Dart* 4A 8
Khalsa Dri. *Grav* 7B 12
Khartoum Pl. *Grav* 6B 12
Killigarth Ct. *Sidc* 4D 14
Kilndown. *Grav* 6C 22
Kimberley Dri. *Sidc* 2G 15
Kinder Clo. *SE28* 1B 2
King Edward Av. *Dart* 6J 7
King Edward Rd. *Grnh* 5H 9
Kingfisher Ct. *W King* 7B 30
Kingfisher Dri. *Grnh* 6H 9
Kingfisher Pl. *S Dar* 2D 26
King Harolds Way.
Bexh & Belv 7B 2
King's Clo. *Dart* 4D 6
Kingsdale Ct. *Swans* 6B 10
Kingsdown Clo. *Grav* 1E 22
Kings Dri. *Grav* 3A 22
Kings Farm. **3B 22**
Kingsfield Ter. *Dart* 5J 7
Kingsgate Clo. *Bexh* 1H 5
Kingsingfield Clo. *W King* 7B 30
Kingsingfield Rd. *W King* 7B 30
Kingsley Av. *Dart* 5B 8
Kingsley Ct. *Bexh* 5K 5
Kingsmead Clo. *Sidc* 2D 14
Kingsridge Gdns. *Dart* 6J 7
Kingston Ct. *N'fleet* 5E 10
King St. *Grav* 6A 12
Kingswood Av. *Belv* 4D 2
Kingswood Av. *Swan* 4E 24
Kingswood Clo. *Dart* 6H 7
Kipling Av. *Til* 1A 12
Kipling Rd. *Bexh* 1H 5
Kipling Rd. *Dart* 5C 8
Kirby Rd. *Dart* 7E 8
Kirkland Clo. *Sidc* 6B 4
Kitchener Av. *Grav* 4B 22
Knatts Valley Rd. *Knat* 6A 30
Knee Hill. *SE2* 4A 2
Kneehill Cres. *SE2* 4A 2
Knightscroft. *New Ash* 3J 31
Knights Mnr. Way. *Dart* 5A 8
Knockhall. **5K 9**
Knockhall Chase. *Grnh* 5J 9
Knockhall Rd. *Grnh* 6J 9
Knole Ga. *Sidc* 3B 14
Knole Rd. *Dart* 7F 7
Knole, The. *Grav* 7H 21
Knoll Rd. *Bex* 7K 5
Knoll Rd. *Sidc* 5E 14
Knowle Av. *Bexh* 7C 2

L

Laburnum Av. *Dart* 1H 17
Laburnum Av. *Swan* 3C 24
Laburnum Gro. *N'fleet* 7G 11
Lacebark Clo. *Sidc* 7C 4
Ladbrooke Cres. *Sidc* 3G 15
Ladds Way. *Swan* 4C 24
Ladyfields. *N'fleet* 4J 21
Ladywood Rd. *Dart* 5F 19
Lagonda Way. *Dart* 4H 7
Lake Footpath. *SE2* 2B 2
Lakeside Clo. *Sidc* 5F 5
Lakeside Way. *SE2* 3B 2
Lakeview Rd. *Well* 4E 4
Lambardes. *New Ash* 3J 31
Lamb Clo. *Til* 2B 12
Lambert Ct. Eri *6G 3*
(off Park Cres.)
Lamorbey. **1C 14**
Lamorbey Clo. *Sidc* 1C 14
Lamorna Av. *Grav* 2C 22
Lamplighters Clo. *Dart* 6A 8
Lancaster Ct. *Grav* 3B 22
Lance Cft. *New Ash* 2J 31
Lancelot Rd. *Well* 4D 4
Lances Clo. *Meop* 7K 29
Landale Gdns. *Dart* 7H 7
Landseer Av. *N'fleet* 3G 21
Lane Av. *Grnh* 6K 9
Lane End. **4E 18**
Lane End. *Bexh* 3A 6
Lanes Av. *N'fleet* 3J 21
Langafel Clo. *Long* 2B 28
Langdale Cres. *Bexh* 7E 2
Langdale Wlk. *N'fleet* 3H 21
Langdon Shaw. *Sidc* 5C 14
Langford Pl. *Sidc* 3D 14
Langlands Dri. *Dart* 5F 19
Langley Rd. *Well* 6A 2
Langmore Ct. *Bexh* 3G 5
Langworth Clo. *Dart* 3J 17
Lanridge Rd. *SE2* 3B 2
Lansbury Cres. *Dart* 5B 8
Lansbury Gdns. *Til* 1K 11
Lansdowne Av. *Bexh* 7B 2
Lansdowne Rd. *Til* 2J 11
Lansdowne Sq. *N'fleet* 6J 11
Lansdown Pl. *N'fleet* 1J 21
Lansdown Rd. *Grav* 1J 21
Lansdown Rd. *Sidc* 3E 14
Lapis Clo. *Grav* 1G 23
Lapwing Clo. *Eri* 2K 3
Lapwings. *Long* 3E 28
Lapwings, The. *Grav* 2C 22
Larch Gro. *Sidc* 1C 14
Larch Rd. *Dart* 7J 7
Larch Wlk. *Swan* 2C 24
Largo Wlk. *Eri* 1D 6
Larkfield Rd. *Sidc* 3C 14
Larkfields. *N'fleet* 3H 21
Larks Fld. *Hart* 4B 28
Larkspur Lodge. *Sidc* 3E 14
Larkswood Clo. *Eri* 1F 7
Larkwell La. *Hart* 4C 28
Larner Rd. *Eri* 7J 3
Latham Clo. *Dart* 2F 19
Latham Rd. *Bexh* 5K 5
Latona Dri. *Grav* 5E 22
Launton Dri. *Bexh* 5G 5
Laura Dri. *Swan* 7F 17
Laurel Av. *Grav* 2B 22
Laurel Clo. *Dart* 1H 17
Laurel Clo. *Sidc* 3D 14
Laurels, The. *Dart* 3H 17
Laurels, The. *Long* 3F 29
Lavender Hill. *Swan* 3C 24
Lavernock Rd. *Bexh* 2K 5
Lavinia Rd. *Dart* 6A 8
Lawford Gdns. *Dart* 5H 7
Lawn Clo. *Swan* 2B 24
Lawn Rd. *Grav* 6F 11
(in two parts)
Lawns, The. *Sidc* 4E 14
Lawrance Sq. *N'fleet* 3J 21
Lawrence Hill Gdns. *Dart* 6H 7
Lawrence Hill Rd. *Dart* 6H 7
Lawrence Rd. *Eri* 7F 3
Lawson Gdns. *Dart* 5J 7
Lawson Rd. *Dart* 4J 7
Laymarsh Clo. *Belv* 3D 2
Leafield La. *Sidc* 3J 15
Leander Dri. *Grav* 4E 22
Leas Grn. *Chst* 6C 14
Leatherbottle Grn. *Eri* 3D 2
Leather Bottle La. *Belv* 4C 2
Lea Va. *Dart* 4C 6
Leckwith Av. *Bexh* 6C 2
Leechcroft Av. *Sidc* 5C 4
Leechcroft Av. *Swan* 3E 24
Leewood Pl. *Swan* 4C 24
Lefa Bus. & Ind. Est. *Sidc* 6G 15
Leicester Rd. *Til* 1J 11
Leigh Pl. *Dart* 4B 18
Leigh Pl. *Well* 2D 4
Leigh Rd. *Grav* 2A 22
Leighton Gdns. *Til* 1K 11
Leith Pk. Rd. *Grav* 1A 22
Lenderyou Ct. Dart *7J 7*
(off Phoenix Pl.)
Lenham Rd. *Bexh* 6D 2
Lennox Av. *Grav* 6J 11
Lennox Ho. Belv *3E 2*
(off Picardy St.)
Lennox Rd. *Grav* 6J 11
Lennox Rd. E. *Grav* 7K 11
Lenor Clo. *Bexh* 4H 5
Lensbury Way. *SE2* 3A 2
Leonard Av. *Swans* 7B 10
Lesley Clo. *Bex* 7A 6
Lesley Clo. *Ist R* 1J 29
Lesley Clo. *Swan* 3C 24
Lesnes Abbey. **4B 2**
Lesney Farm Est. *Eri* 7H 3
Lesney Pk. *Eri* 6H 3
Lesney Pk. Rd. *Eri* 6H 3
Lessness Av. *Bexh* 7B 2
Lessness Heath. **5E 2**
Lessness Pk. *Belv* 5D 2
Lessness Rd. *Belv* 6E 2
Lewin Rd. *Bexh* 5H 5
Lewis Ct. *Grav* 2J 21
Lewis Rd. *Ist R* 1J 29
Lewis Rd. *Sidc* 3F 15
Lewis Rd. *Swans* 6B 10
Lewis Rd. *Well* 3F 5
Leycroft Gdns. *Eri* 1G 7
Leydenhatch La. *Swan* 1B 24
Leyhill Clo. *Swan* 5D 24
Leysdown Av. *Bexh* 4B 6
Leyton Cross. **3F 17**
Leyton Cross Rd. *Dart* 3E 16
Lilac Gdns. *Swan* 3C 24
Lilac Pl. *Meop* 6K 29
Lila Pl. *Swan* 4D 24
Lime Av. *N'fleet* 7G 11
Lime Gro. *Sidc* 6C 4
Lime Rd. *Eri* 3D 2
Lime Rd. *Swan* 3C 24
Lime Row. *Eri* 3D 2
Limes, The. *Dart* 7A 8
Limestone Wlk. *Eri* 2B 2
Lime Tree Av. *Blue* 7H 9
Limetree Ter. *Well* 3D 4
Limewood Rd. *Eri* 7G 3
Lincoln Clo. *Eri* 2E 6
Lincoln Rd. *Eri* 2E 6
(in two parts)
Lincoln Rd. *Sidc* 5E 14
Lincolnshire Ter. *Dart* 4E 18
Linden Av. *Dart* 1H 17
Linden Ct. *Sidc* 4B 14
Lindisfarne Clo. *Grav* 2D 22
Lingey Clo. *Sidc* 2C 14
Lingfield Av. *Dart* 7C 8

Lingfield Cres. SE9 . . . . . .4A 4
Lingfield Rd. Grav 2A 22
Ling Rd. Eri 6G 3
Lingwood. Bexh 2A 6
Links Vw. Dart 1G 17
Link, The. New Ash 3J 31
Linley Clo. E Til 1J 13
Linnet Clo. SE28 . . . . .1A 2
Linton Clo. Well 1E 4
Lion Rd. Bexh 4H 5
LIONS HOSPICE, THE. 4J 21
Liskeard Clo. Chst 6A 14
Lisle Clo. Grav 2G 23
Lister Rd. Til 2K 11
Little Birches. Sidc 2B 14
Littlebrook Bus. Cen. Dart . . .2C 8
LITTLE BROOK HOSPITAL . . .6C 8
Littlebrook Interchange.
    (Junct.) 4C 8
Littlebrook Mnr. Way. Dart . . .5B 8
Littlecroft. Ist R 7H 21
Littledale. Grn St 3D 18
Lit. Heath Rd. Bexh 1J 5
Lit. Queen St. Dart 7A 8
Livingstone Gdns. Grav 5C 22
LIVINGSTONE HOSPITAL. . . .7A 8
Livingstone Rd. Grav 5C 22
Loam Ct. Dart 1K 17
Lochmere Clo. Eri 6F 3
Lodge Av. Dart 6H 7
Lodge Hill. Well . . . . .1E 4 & 7A 2
Lodge La. Bex 6G 5
Lombard St. Hort K 5D 26
Londonderry Pde. Eri 7H 3
London International Cruise
    Terminal. Til 4K 11
London Rd. Cray 5C 6
London Rd. Grnh & Swans . . .5J 9
London Rd. N'fleet 6G 11
London Rd. Stne & Grnh 7C 8
London Rd.
    Swan & F'ham 1B 24
    (in four parts)
London Rd. Til 2A 12
London Rd. W King 5A 30
Longfield. 2B 28
Longfield Av. Long & Grav . . .2F 29
Longfield Hill. 4G 29
Longfield Rd.
    Long & Meop 5G 29
Longlands. 3A 14
Longlands Ct. Sidc 3C 14
Longlands Pk. Cres. Sidc 3B 14
Longlands Rd. Sidc 3B 14
Long La. Bexh 7B 2
Longleigh La. SE2 . . . . .6A 2
Longmarsh Vw. S at H 1C 26
Longmead Dri. Sidc 2G 15
Longmeade. Grav 1E 22
Longmeadow Rd. Sidc 1B 14
Longreach Rd. Eri 2K 3
Longtown Ct. Dart 6C 8
    (off Osbourne Rd.)
Longwalk. Ist R 1H 29
Lonsdale Cres. Dart 1D 18
Lonsdale Rd. Bexh 2J 5
Lord St. Grav 7A 12
Lordswood Clo. Dart 4F 19
Lorton Clo. Grav 2D 22
Lorton Rd. Grav 2C 22
Louvain Rd. Grnh 7F 9
Lovelace Clo. W King 6B 30
Love La. Bex 6J 5
    (in two parts)
Love La. Grav 7B 12
Lovel Av. Well 2D 4
Lovers La. Grnh 4K 9
Low Clo. Grnh 5H 9
Lwr. Church Hill. Grnh 5F 9
Lower Cft. Swan 4E 24
Lwr. Guild Hall. Blue 7G 9
Lwr. Higham Rd. Grav 1E 22
Lwr. Park Rd. Belv 4E 2
Lwr. Range Rd. Grav 7D 12
Lower Rd. Belv 3F 3
Lower Rd. N'fleet 4B 10
    (in two parts)

Lower Rd. Shorne 2K 23
Lower Rd. Swan 7E 16
Lwr. Rose Gallery. Blue 7G 9
Lower Shorne. 4K 23
Lwr. Station Rd. Cray 6D 6
Lwr. Thames Wlk. Blue 1G 19
Lowfield St. Dart 7K 7
Lowry Clo. Eri 4H 3
Lucas Cres. Grnh 4K 9
Lucerne Ct. Eri 3C 2
Luddesdon Rd. Eri 7E 2
Luffield Rd. SE2 . . . . .3A 2
Lullingstone Av. Swan 3E 24
Lullingstone Clo. Orp 7E 14
Lullingstone Cres. Orp 7D 14
Lullingstone Rd. Belv 6D 2
Lulworth Rd. Well 2C 4
Lumley Clo. Belv 5E 2
Lunedale Rd. Dart 2C 18
Luton Rd. Sidc 3F 15
Lydd Clo. Sidc 3B 14
Lydd Rd. Bexh 7D 2
Lydford Ct. Dart 6C 8
    (off Clifton Wlk.)
Lydia Cotts. Grav 7A 12
Lydia Rd. Eri 6K 3
Lyme Rd. Well 1E 4
Lyminge Clo. Sidc 4C 14
Lynden Way. Swan 3B 24
Lyndhurst Clo. Bexh 3A 6
Lyndhurst Rd. Bexh 3A 6
Lyndhurst Way. Ist R 1H 29
Lyndon Av. Sidc 5C 4
Lyndon Rd. Belv 4E 2
Lynmere Rd. Well 2E 4
Lynsted Clo. Bexh 5A 6
Lynton Rd. Grav 1K 21
Lynton Rd. S. Grav 1K 21

M

Mabel Rd. Swan 6F 17
MacArthur Clo. Eri 5J 3
Macaulay Way. SE28 . . . . . . .1A 2
McCudden Rd. Dart 3A 8
Mackenzie Way. Grav 6C 22
McKillop Way. Sidc 7F 15
McLeod Rd. SE2 . . . . .4A 2
McMillan Clo. Grav 4B 22
Macmillan Gdns. Dart 4B 8
Madden Clo. Swans 6A 10
Maddocks Clo. Sidc 5H 15
Madison Cres. Bexh 7A 2
Madison Gdns. Bexh 7A 2
Maida Rd. Belv 3E 2
Maida Va. Rd. Dart 5F 7
Maiden Erlegh Av. Bex 1H 15
Maiden La. Dart 3F 7
Maidstone Rd. Sidc 6G 15
Main Rd. Crock 6C 24
Main Rd. Eyns 6K 25
Main Rd. F'ham 3A 30
Main Rd. Hex 7E 16
Main Rd. Long & Long H 2A 28
Main Rd. Sidc 3A 14
Main Rd. S at H 6C 18
Mallard Clo. Dart 5A 8
Mallard Wlk. Sidc 6F 15
Mallow Clo. N'fleet 4H 21
Mall, The. Bexh 4K 5
Mall, The. Swan 3D 24
Mallys Pl. S Dar 1D 26
Malta Rd. Til 2J 11
Malthouse La. Shorne 5K 23
Malthus Path. SE28 . . . . .1A 2
Maltings Enterprise Cen., The.
    Grav 1E 22
Maltings M. Sidc 3D 14
Maltings, The. Grav 4D 22
    (off Clifton Rd.)
Malvern Av. Bexh 7C 2
Malvern Ho. Grav 6G 11
    (off Laburnum Gro.)
Malvina Av. Grav 2A 22
Malyons Rd. Swan 7E 16
Manford Ind. Est. Eri 1K 3

Mangold Way. Eri 3B 2
Mannock Rd. Dart 3A 8
Manor Clo. Cray 4C 6
Manor Clo. Grav 2G 23
Manor Clo. Wilm 3F 17
Manor Ct. Bexh 4A 6
Manor Dri. Hart 6C 28
Manor Farm. F'ham 6A 26
Manor Forstal. New Ash 3J 31
Manor Ho. New Ash 3J 31
Manor La. Fawk 7K 27
Manor La. Hart 6D 28
Manor Pk. Eri 1J 3
Mnr. Park Rd. Chst 7A 14
Manor Pl. Dart 1K 17
Manor Rd. Bex 1A 16
Manor Rd. Dart 4D 6
Manor Rd. Eri 6K 3
Manor Rd. Grav 6A 12
Manor Rd. Long H 5F 29
Manor Rd. Sidc 3C 14
Manor Rd. Swans 6A 10
Manor Rd. Til 2K 11
Manorside Clo. SE2 . . . . .4A 2
Manor Vw. Hart 6D 28
Manor Way. Bex 1K 15
Manor Way. Bexh 3C 6
Manor Way. Grav 4D 10
Manor Way. Swans 4A 10
Manse Pde. Swan 4F 25
Manse Way. Swan 4F 25
Mansfield Rd. Swan 6D 16
Maple Clo. Swan 2D 24
Maple Ct. Grnh 7F 9
Maple Cres. Sidc 6D 4
Mapledene. Chst 5A 14
Maple Leaf Dri. Sidc 1C 14
Maple Rd. Dart 1H 17
Maple Rd. Grav 4B 22
Maples, The. Long 2E 28
Maplin Ho. SE2 . . . . .2B 2
    (off Wolvercote Rd.)
Maran Way. Eri 3B 2
Marcet Rd. Dart 5H 7
Marconi Rd. N'fleet 3G 21
Marcus Rd. Dart 7F 7
Marden Cres. Bex 5B 6
Marechal Niel Av. Sidc 3A 14
Marechal Niel Pde. Sidc 3A 14
    (off Main Rd.)
Margaret Barr Row.
    Swans 7B 10
Margaret Rd. Bex 6G 5
Marina Dri. Dart 1B 18
Marina Dri. N'fleet 7J 11
Marina Dri. Well 2B 4
Marine Ct. Eri 7K 3
Mariners Ct. Grnh 4J 9
Mariners Wlk. Eri 6K 3
Mariners Way. N'fleet 7H 11
Maritime Clo. Grnh 5J 9
Maritime Ga. N'fleet 7H 11
Mark Clo. Bexh 1H 5
Market All. Grav 6A 12
Market Pde. Sidc 4E 14
Market Pl. Bexh 4K 5
Market Pl. Dart 7K 7
Market Pl. Til 2K 11
Market St. Dart 7K 7
Mark La. Grav 7D 12
    (in two parts)
Marks Sq. N'fleet 4J 21
Mark Way. Swan 5F 25
Marlborough Pk. Av. Sidc 7D 4
Marlborough Rd. Bexh 3G 5
Marlborough Rd. Dart 6H 7
Marler Ho. Eri 2E 6
Marley Av. Bexh 6B 2
Marling Way. Grav 6D 22
Marlowe Rd. Chst 6A 14
Marlowes, The. Dart 4C 6
Marlwood Clo. Sidc 2B 14
Marne Av. Well 3D 4
Marrabon Clo. Sidc 1D 14
Marriott Rd. Dart 7A 8
Marriotts Wharf. Grav 5A 12

Marsham Ho. Eri 2B 2
Marsh St. Dart 2B 8
    (in three parts)
Marsh Vw. Grav 1E 22
Martens Av. Bexh 4A 6
Martens Clo. Bexh 4B 6
Martin Dene. Bexh 5J 5
Martin Dri. Stne 7D 8
Martin Ho. Grav 3K 21
Martin Ri. Bexh 5J 5
Martin Rd. Dart 3H 17
Marwood Clo. Well 3E 4
Maryfield Clo. Bex 3D 16
Maryville. Well 2C 4
Masefield Clo. Eri 1E 6
Masefield Rd. Dart 5C 8
Masefield Rd. N'fleet 3G 21
Mason Clo. Bexh 3A 6
Masthead Clo. Dart 4D 8
Matfield Rd. Belv 6E 2
Maude Rd. Swan 6F 17
Maximfeldt Rd. Eri 5J 3
Maxim Rd. Dart 5D 6
Maxim Rd. Eri 4J 3
Maxwell Rd. Well 3C 4
May Av. N'fleet 1J 21
May Av. Ind. Est. N'fleet 1J 21
    (off May Av.)
Maybury Av. Dart 1D 18
Mayes Clo. Swan 4F 25
Mayfair Av. Bexh 1G 5
Mayfair Rd. Dart 5J 7
Mayfield. Bexh 3J 5
Mayfield Rd. Belv 4G 3
Mayfield Rd. Grav 7J 11
Mayfields. Swans 6B 10
Maylands Dri. Sidc 3G 15
Maynard Clo. Eri 7K 3
Mayor's La. Dart 4H 17
Mayplace Av. Dart 4F 7
Mayplace Clo. Bexh 3A 6
Mayplace Rd. E. Bexh 3A 6
Mayplace Rd. W. Bexh 4K 5
Maypole. 1D 16
Maypole Rd. Grav 1E 22
May Rd. Dart 4A 18
Mead Clo. Swan 5F 25
Mead Cres. Dart 1J 17
Meadow Bank Clo.
    W King 7C 30
Meadow Clo. Bexh 5J 5
Meadow La. New Ash 2J 31
Meadow Rd. Grav 2K 21
Meadow Rd. N'fleet 1F 21
Meadows Ct. Sidc 6E 14
Meadowside. Dart 1J 17
Meadow Vw. Sidc 7E 4
Meadowview Rd. Bex 6H 5
Meadow Wlk. Dart 4H 17
    (in two parts)
Mead Rd. Dart 7D 8
Mead Rd. Eri 1J 17
Mead Rd. Grav 2A 22
Mead, The. New Ash 2H 31
Medbury Rd. Grav 1E 22
Medhurst Cres. Grav 3D 22
Medhurst Gdns. Grav 3E 22
Medina Ho. Eri 7J 3
Medlar Ho. Sidc 3D 14
Medlars, The. Meop 6K 29
Medway Rd. Dart 3F 7
Melanie Clo. Bexh 1H 5
Melba Gdns. Til 1K 11
Melbourne Ct. Grav 6A 12
Melbourne Rd. Til 1H 11
Melliker La. Meop 6J 29
Melrose Av. Dart 6D 6
Melville Rd. Sidc 2F 15
Mendip Rd. Bexh 1D 6
Meopham. 7K 29
Meopham Station. 5K 29
Mera Dri. Bexh 4K 5
Merchland Rd. SE9 . . . . .1A 14
Merewood Rd. Bexh 2B 6
Merino Pl. Sidc 6D 4
Merleys Clo. Long 3F 29
Merlin Rd. Well 4D 4

Merlin Rd. N. *Well* 4D **4**
Mermerus Gdns. *Grav* 4E **22**
Merrilees Rd. *Sidc* 1B **14**
Merryfields Clo. *Hart* 4C **28**
Merryweather Clo. *Dart* 6A **8**
Merton Av. *Hart* 4B **28**
Merton Ct. *Well* 2E **4**
Methuen Rd. *Belv* 4F **3**
Methuen Rd. *Bexh* 4J **5**
Mews, The. *Hart* 3B **28**
Mews, The. *Sidc* 4D **14**
Meyer Rd. *Eri* 6H **3**
Michael Gdns. *Grav* 6D **22**
Michaels La. *Fawk & Sev* . . .2E **30**
Middleham Ct. Dart 6C **8**
(off Osbourne Rd.)
Middleton Av. *Sidc* 6E **14**
Middle Way. *Eri* 3C **2**
Midfield Av. *Bexh* 3B **6**
Midfield Av. *Swan* 6F **17**
Midfield Pde. *Bexh* 3B **6**
Midfield Way. *Orp* 7E **14**
Midhurst Hill. *Bexh* 6K **5**
Midwinter Clo. *Well* 3D **4**
Mike Spring Ct. *Grav* 4C **22**
Mildred Clo. *Dart* 6B **8**
Mildred Rd. *Eri* 5J **3**
Mile End Green. 1A **28**
Milestone Rd. *Dart* 6C **8**
Milford Clo. *SE2* 6C **2**
Millbro. *Swan* 1F **25**
Millbrook Av. *Well* 4A **4**
Mill Ct. *Hort K* 2C **26**
Miller Ct. *Bexh* 3B **6**
Miller Rd. *Grav* 2F **23**
Millfield. *New Ash* 2H **31**
Millfield Dri. *N'fleet* 2H **21**
Millfield La. *New Ash* 2H **31**
Millfield Rd. *W King* 6A **30**
Mill Hill La. *Shorne* 5J **23**
Mill Pl. *Dart* 4F **7**
Mill Pond Rd. *Dart* 6K **7**
Mill Rd. *Dart* 4A **18**
Mill Rd. *Eri* 7G **3**
Mill Rd. *N'fleet* 7H **11**
Mill Row. *Bex* 1A **16**
Millside Ind. Est. *Dart* 4J **7**
Mill Stone Clo. *S Dar* 2D **26**
Mill Stone M. *S Dar* 1D **26**
Milner Wlk. *Sidc* 2A **14**
Milroy Av. *N'fleet* 2H **21**
Milton. 7B **12**
Milton Av. *Grav* 1B **22**
Milton Ct. *Grav* 1B **22**
Milton Gdns. *Til* 1A **12**
Milton Hall Rd. *Grav* 1C **22**
Milton Lodge. *Sidc* 4D **14**
Milton Pl. *Grav* 6B **12**
Milton Rd. *Belv* 4E **2**
Milton Rd. *Grav* 6A **12**
(in two parts)
Milton Rd. *Swans* 6B **10**
Milton Rd. *Well* 1C **4**
Milton Rd. Bus. Pk. Grav 7B **12**
(off Milton Rd.)
Milton St. *Swans* 6A **10**
Minerva Clo. *Sidc* 4B **14**
Minnis, The. *New Ash* 3J **31**
Minshaw Ct. *Sidc* 4C **14**
Miskin Rd. *Dart* 7H **7**
Miskin Way. *Grav* 6C **22**
Mitchell Av. *N'fleet* 2G **21**
Mitchell Clo. *SE2* 4A **2**
Mitchell Clo. *Belv* 3G **3**
Mitchell Clo. *Dart* 2K **17**
Mitchell Wlk. *Swans* 7B **10**
Mitcham Clo. *W King* 7B **30**
Moat Ct. *Sidc* 3C **14**
Moat Cft. *Well* 3F **5**
Moat La. *Eri* 1F **7**
Mollison Ri. *Grav* 5D **22**
Monarch Clo. *Til* 2A **12**
Monarch Rd. *Belv* 3E **2**
Monica James Ho. *Sidc* 3D **14**
Monks Clo. *SE2* 4B **2**
Monks Orchard. *Dart* 2H **17**
Monks Wlk. *S'fleet* 6D **20**

Monkton Rd. *Well* 2C **4**
Monmouth Clo. *Well* 4D **4**
Montague Rd. *Sidc* 3D **14**
Montague Pl. *Swan* 4E **24**
Monterey Clo. *Bex* 2B **16**
Montgomery Clo. *Sidc* 6C **4**
Montgomery Rd. *S Dar* 1E **26**
Montpelier Av. *Bex* 7G **5**
Montreal Rd. *Til* 3K **11**
Montrose Av. *Sidc* 7D **4**
Montrose Av. *Well* 3A **4**
Montrose Clo. *Well* 3C **4**
Moore Av. *Til* 2A **12**
Moore Clo. *Dart* 2E **18**
Moore Rd. *Swans* 6B **10**
Moorhen Clo. *Eri* 2K **3**
Morello Clo. *Swan* 4C **24**
Moreton Clo. *Swan* 2D **24**
Moreton Ct. *Dart* 3E **6**
Moreton Ind. Est. *Swan* 4G **25**
Morgan Dri. *Grnh* 7E **8**
Morland Av. *Dart* 5G **7**
Mornington Ct. *Bex* 1C **16**
Morris Gdns. *Dart* 5B **8**
Mortimer Rd. *Eri* 6H **3**
Morvale Clo. *Belv* 4D **2**
Mossdown Clo. *Belv* 4E **2**
Moss Way. *Dart* 4E **18**
Mote, The. *New Ash* 2J **31**
Mottisfont Rd. *SE2* 3A **2**
Moultain Hill. *Swan* 4F **25**
Mt. Culver Av. *Sidc* 6G **15**
Mount Dri. *Bexh* 5H **5**
Mountjoy Clo. *SE2* 2A **2**
Mt. Pleasant Rd. *Dart* 6A **8**
Mt. Pleasant Wlk. *Bex* 5B **6**
Mount Rd. *Dart* 6E **6**
Mounts Rd. *Bexh* 5G **5**
Mounts Rd. *Grnh* 5J **9**
Mount, The. *Bexh* 5A **6**
Muggins La. *Shorne* 4H **23**
Mulberry Clo. *Meop* 6K **29**
Mulberry Rd. *N'fleet* 3H **21**
Mulberry Way. *Belv* 2G **3**
Mullender Ct. *Grav* 1F **23**
Multon Rd. *W King* 6B **30**
Munford Dri. *Swans* 7B **10**
Mungo Pk. Rd. *Grav* 5C **22**
Murchison Av. *Bex* 1G **15**
Muscovy Ho. Eri 3C **2**
(off Kale Rd.)
Mussenden La.
    Hort K & Fawk 5D **26**
Myrtle Clo. *Eri* 1D **6**
Myrtle Pl. *Dart* 7E **8**
Myrtle Rd. *Dart* 1J **17**

N

Nags Head La. *Well* 3E **4**
Nairn Ct. *Til* 2J **11**
Nansen Rd. *Grav* 4C **22**
Napier Rd. *Belv* 4D **2**
Napier Rd. *N'fleet* 1J **21**
Naseby Ct. *Sidc* 4C **14**
Nash Bank. *Meop* 2J **29**
Nash Cft. *N'fleet* 4H **21**
Nash Street. 2K **29**
Nash St. *Meop* 2J **29**
Nassau Path. *SE28* 1A **2**
Neal Rd. *W King* 6B **30**
Nelson Ct. Eri 7K **3**
(off Frobisher Rd.)
Nelson Ho. *Grnh* 5K **9**
Nelson Pl. *Sidc* 4D **14**
Nelson Rd. *Belv* 5D **2**
Nelson Rd. *Dart* 6H **7**
Nelson Rd. *N'fleet* 2J **21**
Nelson Rd. *Sidc* 4D **14**
Neptune Ct. Eri 7K **3**
(off Frobisher Rd.)
Neptune Wlk. *Eri* 4H **3**
Nethewode Ct. Belv 3F **3**
(off Lwr. Park Rd.)
Neville Clo. *Sidc* 4C **14**
Nevill Pl. *Meop* 5K **29**

New Ash Green. 2J **31**
New Barn. 3F **28**
New Barn Rd.
    S'fleet & Long 3F **21**
New Barn Rd. *Swan* 1D **24**
Newbery Rd. *Eri* 1E **6**
Newbury Ct. *Sidc* 4C **14**
New House. 3J **21**
New Ho. La.
    Grav & N'fleet 3J **21**
Newick Clo. *Bex* 6A **6**
Newlyn Rd. *Well* 2C **4**
Newmans Rd. *N'fleet* 2J **21**
Newnham Lodge. *Belv* 5E **2**
(off Erith Rd.)
Newports. *Swan* 7C **24**
New Rd. *SE2* 4B **2**
New Rd. *Grav* 6K **11**
New Rd. *Hex* 7E **16**
New Rd. *Meop* 5J **29**
New Rd. *S Dar* 2D **26**
New Rd. *Swan* 3E **24**
New Rd. *Well* 2E **4**
New Swan Yd. *Grav* 6A **12**
New Tavern Fort. 6B **12**
(off Commercial Pl.)
Newton Abbot Rd. *N'fleet* . . .2J **21**
Newton Rd. *Til* 3K **11**
Newton Rd. *Well* 3D **4**
Newtons Ct. *Dart* 4E **8**
New Town. 6B **8**
Nichola Ter. *Bexh* 1H **5**
Nickleby Rd. *Grav* 1F **23**
Nightingale Clo. *N'fleet* 3H **21**
Nightingale Gro. *Dart* 4B **8**
Nightingale Way. *Swan* 3D **24**
Nine Elms Gro. *Grav* 7K **11**
Noel Ter. *Sidc* 4E **14**
Nordenfeldt Rd. *Eri* 5H **3**
Norfield Rd. *Dart* 4B **16**
Norfolk Clo. *Dart* 6B **8**
Norfolk Cres. *Sidc* 7B **4**
Norfolk Gdns. *Bexh* 1J **5**
Norfolk Pl. *Well* 2D **4**
Norfolk Rd. *Grav* 6C **12**
(in two parts)
Norham Ct. Dart 6C **8**
(off Osbourne Rd.)
Normandy Way. *Eri* 1D **6**
Normanhurst Av. *Bexh* 1G **5**
Norman Pde. *Sidc* 2G **15**
Norman Rd. *Belv* 3F **3**
(in two parts)
Norman Rd. *Dart* 1K **17**
Norman's Clo. *Grav* 7K **11**
Norris Way. *Dart* 3E **6**
Northall Rd. *Bexh* 2B **6**
N. Ash Rd. *New Ash* 3H **31**
North Clo. *Bexh* 4G **5**
Northcote Rd. *Grav* 1J **21**
Northcote Rd. *Sidc* 8B **14**
North Cray. 5H **15**
N. Cray Rd. *Sidc & Bex* 6H **15**
Northdown Rd. *Long* 2A **28**
Northdown Rd. *Well* 2E **4**
North End. 1E **6**
Northend Rd. *Eri* 7K **3**
Northend Trad. Est. *Eri* 1D **6**
Northfield. *Hart* 3C **28**
Northfleet. 6E **10**
Northfleet Green. 5F **21**
Northfleet Grn. Rd. *S'fleet* . . .6F **21**
Northfleet Ind. Est. *N'fleet* . . .4C **10**
N. Glade, The. *Bex* 7J **5**
N. Kent Av. *N'fleet* 6F **11**
N. Ridge Rd. *Grav* 3B **22**
North Riding. *Hart* 3G **29**
North Rd. *Belv* 3F **3**
North Rd. *Dart* 6E **6**
North Sq. *New Ash* 2J **31**
North St. *Bexh* 4K **5**
North St. *Dart* 5G **7**
North St. *Grav* 7A **12**
Northumberland Av. *Well* 4A **4**
Northumberland Clo. *Eri* 7G **3**
Northumberland Heath. 7G **3**
Northumberland Pk. *Eri* 7G **3**

Northumberland Rd. *Ist R* . . .7J **21**
Northumberland Way. *Eri* 1B **6**
Northview. *Swan* 2D **24**
N. View Av. *Til* 1K **11**
Northwood Pl. *Eri* 3D **2**
Norvic Ho. *Eri* 7K **3**
Norwich Pl. *Bexh* 4K **5**
Norwood Ct. Dart 5B **8**
(off Farnol Rd.)
Norwood La. *Meop* 5K **29**
Nuffield Rd. *Swan* 6F **17**
Nursery Av. *Bexh* 3J **5**
Nursery Clo. *Dart* 7D **8**
Nursery Clo. *Swan* 2B **24**
Nursery Rd. *Meop* 5K **29**
Nursery, The. *Eri* 7K **3**
Nurstead. 3J **29**
Nurstead Av. *Long* 4G **29**
Nurstead Chu. La. *Meop* 4J **29**
Nurstead La. *Long H* 4G **29**
Nurstead Rd. *Eri* 7E **2**
Nuthatch. *Long* 3E **28**
Nutley Clo. *Swan* 1E **24**
Nutmead Clo. *Bex* 1B **16**
Nuxley Rd. *Belv* 6D **2**

O

Oak Clo. *Dart* 4D **6**
Oakdene Av. *Eri* 6G **3**
Oakenholt Ho. *SE2* 1B **2**
Oakfield La. *Dart* 2D **16**
Oakfield Pk. Rd. *Dart* 2J **17**
Oakfield Pl. *Dart* 2J **17**
Oakhouse Rd. *Bexh* 5K **5**
Oakhurst Av. *Bexh* 7C **2**
Oakhurst Gdns. *Bexh* 7C **2**
Oaklands Av. *Sidc* 7C **4**
Oaklands Clo. *Bexh* 5J **5**
Oaklands Clo. *W King* 6B **30**
Oaklands Rd. *Bexh* 4J **5**
Oaklands Rd. *Dart* 1C **18**
Oaklands Rd. *N'fleet* 4J **21**
Oakleigh Clo. *Swan* 3D **24**
Oakley Dri. *SE9* 1A **14**
Oakley Pk. *Bex* 7F **5**
Oak Rd. *Eri* 6H **5**
(Mill Rd.)
Oak Rd. *Eri* 2F **7**
(Moat La.)
Oak Rd. *Grav* 3B **22**
Oak Rd. *Grnh* 6C **8**
Oaks, The. *Dart* 6C **8**
Oaks, The. *Swan* 2D **24**
Oak Tree Av. *Blue* 7G **9**
Oakway Clo. *Bex* 6H **5**
Oakwood Clo. *Dart* 1C **18**
Oakwood Ct. Swan 2B **24**
(off Lawn Clo.)
Oakwood Dri. *Bexh* 4B **6**
Oakwood Ri. *Long* 3B **28**
Oast Way. *Hart* 6B **28**
Ockham Dri. *Orp* 7D **14**
Ockley Ct. *Sidc* 3B **14**
Okehampton Cres. *Well* 1E **4**
Old Barn Way. *Bexh* 3C **6**
Old Bexley. 7A **6**
Old Bexley Bus. Pk. *Bex* 7A **6**
Old Bexley La. *Bex & Dart* . . .2C **16**
(in two parts)
Old Chapel Rd. *Swan* 7B **24**
Old Dartford Rd. *F'ham* 6A **26**
Old Downs. *Hart* 5B **28**
Old Farm Av. *Sidc* 1A **14**
Old Farm Gdns. *Swan* 3E **24**
Old Farm Rd. E. *Sidc* 2D **14**
Old Farm Rd. W. *Sidc* 2C **14**
Oldfield Rd. *Bexh* 2H **5**
Old Forge Way. *Sidc* 4E **14**
Old London Rd. *Sidc* 7K **15**
Old Maidstone Rd. *Sidc* 7J **15**
Old Mnr. Dri. *Grav* 1B **22**
Old Mnr. Way. *Bexh* 2C **6**
Old Parsonage Yd., The.
    Hort K 4D **26**
Old Perry St. *Chst* 6B **14**

Old Perry St. *N'fleet* 2H **21**
Old Rd. *Dart* 5C **6**
Old Rd. E. *Grav* 1A **22**
Old Rd. W. *Grav* 1J **21**
Old Watling St. *Grav* 5K **21**
Old Yews, The. *Long* 3E **28**
Oliver Clo. *Grays* 1G **9**
Oliver Cres. *F'ham* 7A **26**
Olive Rd. *Dart* 1J **17**
Oliver Rd. *Grays* 1G **9**
Oliver Rd. *Swan* 3C **24**
Olivers Mill. *New Ash* 2H **31**
Olron Cres. *Bexh* 5G **5**
Olyffe Av. *Well* 1D **4**
Onslow Dri. *Sidc* 2G **15**
Orbital One. *Dart* 2C **18**
Orbital One Ind. Est. *Dart* . . .2B **18**
Orchard Av. *Belv* 6C **2**
Orchard Av. *Dart* 7G **7**
Orchard Av. *Grav* 5A **22**
Orchard Clo. *Bexh* 1H **5**
Orchard Clo. *Long* 2E **28**
Orchard Dri. *Meop* 5J **29**
Orchard Hill. *Dart* 5D **6**
Orchard Ho. *Eri* 1E **6**
Orchard Lea. *S'fleet* 5C **20**
Orchard Ri. E. *Sidc* 5B **4**
Orchard Ri. W. *Sidc* 5B **4**
Orchard Rd. *Belv* 4E **2**
Orchard Rd. *N'fleet* 2F **21**
Orchard Rd. *Sidc* 4B **14**
Orchard Rd. *Swans* 5B **10**
Orchard Rd. *Well* 3E **4**
Orchards Shop. Cen., The.
   Dart 6K **7**
Orchards, The. *Dart* 6K **7**
Orchard St. *Dart* 6K **7**
Orchard, The. *Swan* 2C **24**
Orchard Theatre. **6K 7**
Orchard Way. *Dart* 3J **17**
Ordnance Rd. *Grav* 6B **12**
Orford Ct. Dart 6C **8**
   (off Osbourne Rd.)
Orlick Rd. *Grav* 1G **23**
Osborne Rd. *Belv* 5D **2**
Osbourne Rd. *Dart* 6C **8**
Osney Ho. *SE2* 2B **2**
Osney Way. *Grav* 2E **22**
Osterberg Rd. *Dart* 4A **8**
Otford Clo. *Bex* 6A **6**
Ottawa Rd. *Til* 2K **11**
Oval, The. *Long* 3F **29**
Oval, The. *Sidc* 7D **4**
Overcliffe. *Grav* 6K **11**
Overcourt Clo. *Sidc* 6E **4**
Overmead. *SE9* 7A **4**
Overmead. *Swan* 5D **24**
Over Minnis. *New Ash* 3J **31**
Overton Rd. *SE2* 3A **2**
Overton Rd. E. *SE2* 3B **2**
Overy St. *Dart* 6K **7**
Owen Clo. *SE28* 1A **2**
Owenite St. *SE2* 4A **2**
Oxford Clo. *Grav* 2E **22**
Oxford M. *Bex* 7K **5**
Oxford Rd. *Sidc* 5E **14**
Oxleas Clo. *Well* 2A **4**

P

Pacific Clo. *Swans* 5B **10**
Packham Rd. *N'fleet* 3J **21**
Packmores Rd. *SE9* 5A **4**
Paddock Clo. *S Dar* 1D **26**
Paddock Rd. *Bexh* 4H **5**
Paddock Way. *Chst* 7A **14**
Pageant Clo. *Til* 1B **12**
Page Clo. *Bean* 3K **19**
Page Cres. *Eri* 7K **3**
Painters Ash La. *N'fleet* 3G **21**
Palmar Cres. *Bexh* 3K **5**
Palmar Rd. *Bexh* 2K **5**
Palm Av. *Sidc* 6G **15**
Palmeira Rd. *Bexh* 3G **5**
Palmer Av. *Grav* 4C **22**

Panter's. *Swan* 7E **16**
Pantiles, The. *Bexh* 7D **2**
Parade, The. *Dart* 5E **6**
Parade, The. *Grav* 2C **22**
Parade, The. *Meop* 7K **29**
Parade, The. *Swans* 5C **10**
Parish Ga. Dri. *Sidc* 6B **4**
Park App. *Well* 4E **4**
Park Av. *Grav* 1B **22**
Park Av. *N'fleet* 1H **21**
Pk. Corner Rd. *S'fleet* 4C **20**
Park Cres. *Eri* 6G **3**
Park Cres. Rd. *Eri* 6H **3**
Park Dri. *Long* 3B **28**
Parker Av. *Til* 1B **12**
Park Ind. Cen. *Dart* 7D **8**
Parkfield. *Hart* 4B **28**
Park Gdns. *Eri* 4H **3**
Park Gro. *Bexh* 4B **6**
Park Hill. *Meop* 4H **29**
Parkhill Rd. *Bex* 7J **5**
Pk. Hill Rd. *Sidc* 3A **14**
Parkhurst Gdns. *Bex* 7K **5**
Parkhurst Rd. *Bex* 7K **5**
Park La. *Swan* 2H **25**
Park Mead. *Sidc* 5E **4**
Park Pl. *Grav* 6B **12**
Park Rd. *Dart* 7B **8**
Park Rd. *Grav* 1A **22**
Park Rd. *Swan* 4E **24**
Park Rd. *Swans* 6B **10**
Park Rd. Ind. Est. *Swan* 3E **24**
Parkside. *Sidc* 2E **14**
Parkside Av. *Bexh* 2C **6**
Parkside Av. *Til* 2A **12**
Parkside Cross. *Bexh* 2D **6**
Parkside Lodge. *Belv* 5G **3**
Parkside Pde. Dart 2E **6**
   (off Northend Rd.)
Parkside Rd. *Belv* 4F **3**
Park Ter. *Grnh* 5K **9**
Park, The. *Sidc* 5D **14**
Parkview. *Eri* 3B **2**
Pk. View Rd. *Well* 3F **5**
Park Way. *Bex* 3D **16**
Parkway. *Eri* 3C **2**
Pk. Wood Rd. *Bex* 7J **5**
Paroma Rd. *Belv* 3E **2**
Parrock Av. *Grav* 1B **22**
Parrock Farm. **4C 22**
Parrock Rd. *Grav* 1B **22**
Parrock St. *Grav* 6A **12**
Parrock, The. *Grav* 1B **22**
Parsonage La. *Sidc* 4J **15**
Parsonage La. *S at H* 6C **18**
Parsonage Manorway.
   Belv 6E **2**
Parsons La. *Dart* 3G **17**
Partridge Rd. *Sidc* 3B **14**
Patricia Ct. *Well* 1E **4**
Patterdale Rd. *Dart* 1E **18**
Patterson Ct. *Dart* 5B **8**
Peach Cft. *N'fleet* 3G **21**
Peacock St. *Grav* 7B **12**
Peareswood Rd. *Eri* 1E **6**
Pearson Way. *Dart* 2A **18**
Peartree Clo. *Eri* 1C **6**
Pear Tree Clo. *Swan* 2C **24**
Peartree La. *Shorne* 7K **23**
Pease Hill. *Ash* 6H **31**
Peatfield Clo. *Sidc* 3B **14**
Pedham Pl. Ind. Est.
   Swan 5F **25**
Pegasus Ct. *Grav* 3B **22**
Pelham Cotts. *Bex* 1A **16**
Pelham Ct. *Sidc* 3D **14**
Pelham Rd. *Bexh* 3K **5**
Pelham Rd. *Grav* 1J **21**
Pelham Rd. S. *Grav* 1J **21**
Pelham Ter. *Grav* 7J **11**
Pemberton Gdns. *Swan* 3D **24**
Pembroke Pde. *Eri* 5G **3**
Pembroke Pl. *S at H* 1C **26**
Pembroke Rd. *Eri* 5G **3**
Pembury Cres. *Sidc* 2H **15**
Pembury Rd. *Bexh* 7C **2**
Pencroft Dri. *Dart* 7H **7**

Penda Rd. *Eri* 7F **3**
Penenden. *New Ash* 2J **31**
Penfold La. *Bex* 2G **15**
   (in two parts)
Pengarth Rd. *Bex* 5G **5**
Penhill Rd. *Bex* 6F **5**
Penney Clo. *Dart* 7J **7**
Pennine Way. *Bexh* 1D **6**
Pennine Way. *N'fleet* 3H **21**
Pennis La. *Fawk* 6A **28**
Penn La. *Bex* 5G **5**
   (in two parts)
Penpool La. *Well* 3E **4**
Penshurst Av. *Sidc* 6D **4**
Penshurst Clo. *Long* 2G **29**
Penshurst Clo. *W King* 6B **30**
Penshurst Rd. *Bexh* 1J **5**
Penton Ho. *SE2* 1B **2**
Pentstemon Dri. *Swans* 5B **10**
Penventon Ct. Til 2K **11**
   (off Dock Rd.)
Pepper Hill. **3F 21**
Pepperhill. *N'fleet* 3F **21**
Pepperhill La. *N'fleet* 3F **21**
Pepys Clo. *Dart* 4B **8**
Pepys Clo. *N'fleet* 3G **21**
Pepys Clo. *Til* 1B **12**
Percy Rd. *Bexh* 2H **5**
Peregrine Ct. *Well* 1C **4**
Perkins Clo. *Grnh* 5G **9**
Perpins Rd. *SE9* 6A **4**
Perran Clo. *Hart* 4C **28**
Perry Gro. *Dart* 4B **8**
Perry Street. **1J 21**
Perry St. *Chst* 6A **14**
Perry St. *Dart* 4D **6**
Perry St. *N'fleet* 1H **21**
Perry St. Gdns. *Chst* 6B **14**
Perry St. Shaw. *Chst* 7B **14**
Perth Ho. *Til* 2K **11**
Pescot Av. *Long* 3D **28**
Peters Clo. *Well* 2B **4**
Peterstone Rd. *SE2* 2A **2**
Peter St. *Grav* 7A **12**
Petworth Rd. *Bexh* 5K **5**
Peveril Ct. Dart 6C **6**
   (off Clifton Wlk.)
Phelps Clo. *W King* 6B **30**
Philip Av. *Swan* 4C **24**
Phillips Clo. *Dart* 6G **7**
Phoenix Pl. *Dart* 7J **7**
Picardy Manorway. *Belv* 3F **3**
Picardy Rd. *Belv* 5E **2**
Picardy St. *Belv* 3E **2**
Pickering Ct. Dart 6C **8**
   (off Osbourne Rd.)
Pickford Clo. *Bexh* 2H **5**
Pickford La. *Bexh* 2H **5**
Pickford Rd. *Bexh* 3H **5**
Pickwick Gdns. *N'fleet* 3G **21**
Pickwick Ho. *Grav* 3G **21**
Pickwick Way. *Chst* 6A **14**
Pier Rd. *Eri* 6J **3**
   (in two parts)
Pier Rd. *Grnh* 4J **9**
Pier Rd. *N'fleet* 6J **11**
Pilgrim's Ct. *Dart* 5B **8**
Pilgrims Rd. *Swans* 4B **10**
Pilgrims Vw. *Grnh* 6K **9**
Pilgrims Way. *Dart* 1B **18**
Pilots Pl. *Grav* 6B **12**
Pincott Rd. *Bexh* 5K **5**
Pincroft Wood. *Long* 3F **29**
Pinden. **2K 27**
Pine Av. *Grav* 1C **22**
Pine Clo. *Swan* 4E **24**
Pine Ri. *Meop* 6K **29**
Pinewood Av. *Sidc* 1B **14**
Pinewood Rd. *SE2* 6B **2**
Pink's Hill. *Swan* 5D **24**
Pinnacle Hill. *Bexh* 4A **6**
Pinnacle Hill N. *Bexh* 3A **6**
Pinnocks Av. *Grav* 1A **22**
Pioneer Way. *Swan* 3D **24**
Pippins, The. *Meop* 6K **29**
Pirrip Clo. *Grav* 1E **22**
Pitfield. *Hart* 4C **28**

Plane Av. *N'fleet* 7G **11**
Plantation Clo. *Grnh* 6G **9**
Plantation Rd. *Eri* 1F **7**
Plantation Rd. *Swan* 7F **17**
Plaxtol Rd. *Eri* 7E **2**
Pleasant Vw. *Eri* 5J **3**
Plympton Clo. *Belv* 3C **2**
Plymstock Rd. *Well* 7A **2**
Pollard Wlk. *Sidc* 6F **15**
Pondfield La. *Shorne* 7K **23**
Poplar Av. *Grav* 4B **22**
Poplar Mt. *Belv* 4F **3**
Poplar Pl. *SE28* 1A **2**
Poplars Clo. *Long* 3F **29**
Poplars, The. *Grav* 7D **12**
Poplar Wlk. *Meop* 6K **29**
Poppy Clo. *Belv* 3F **3**
Porchester Clo. *Hart* 4C **28**
Porchfield Clo. *Grav* 2B **22**
Port Av. *Grnh* 6J **9**
Porthkerry Av. *Well* 4D **4**
Portland Av. *Grav* 2A **22**
Portland Av. *Sidc* 6D **4**
Portland Rd. *Grav* 1A **22**
Portman Clo. *Bex* 1D **16**
Portman Clo. *Bexh* 3H **5**
Portmeadow Wlk.
   SE2 . . . . .2B **2**
Portsea Rd. *Til* 1B **12**
Pottery Rd. *Bex* 2B **16**
Pound Bank Clo.
   W King 7C **30**
Pound Grn. *Bex* 7K **5**
Pound Way. *Chst* 7A **14**
Powder Mill La. *Dart* 2K **17**
Powell Av. *Dart* 2F **19**
Powerscroft Rd. *Sidc* 6F **15**
Power Works. *Eri* 1F **7**
Powys Clo. *Bexh* 6B **2**
Poynder Rd. *Til* 1A **12**
Poyntell Cres. *Chst* 7A **14**
Preston Ct. Sidc 4C **14**
   (off Crescent, The)
Preston Dri. *Bexh* 1G **5**
Preston Rd. *N'fleet* 1H **21**
Pretoria Ho. *Eri* 7J **3**
Priestlands Pk. Rd. *Sidc* 3C **14**
Priest Wlk. *Grav* 2F **23**
Primmett Clo. *W King* 6B **30**
Primrose Ter. *Grav* 1B **22**
Prince Charles Av. *S Dar* 2E **26**
Princes Av. *Dart* 1C **18**
Princes Clo. *Sidc* 3G **15**
Princes Rd. *Dart* 6F **7**
   (in four parts)
Princes Rd. *Grav* 4B **22**
Princes Rd. *Swan* 6F **17**
Princes Road Interchange.
   (Junct.) **1B 18**
Princesses Pde. Dart 5D **6**
   (off Waterside)
Princess Margaret Rd.
   Linf & E Til 1J **13**
Princes St. *Bexh* 3J **5**
Princes St. *Grav* 6A **12**
   (in two parts)
Princes Vw. *Dart* 1B **18**
Priory Clo. *Dart* 5H **7**
Priory Ct. *Dart* 6J **7**
Priory Dri. *SE2* 5B **2**
Priory Gdns. *Dart* 5J **7**
Priory Hill. *Dart* 5J **7**
Priory Pl. *Dart* 6J **7**
Priory Rd. N. *Dart* 4J **7**
Priory Rd. S. *Dart* 6J **7**
Priory Shop. Cen. *Dart* 6J **7**
Prospect Clo. *Belv* 4E **2**
Prospect Gro. *Grav* 7C **12**
Prospect Pl. *Dart* 6K **7**
Prospect Pl. *Grav* 7C **12**
   (in two parts)
Providence St. *Grnh* 5H **9**
Prudhoe Ct. Dart 6C **8**
   (off Osbourne Rd.)
Puddledock. **5D 16**
Puddledock La. *Dart* 5D **16**
Punch Cft. *New Ash* 3H **31**

Q

Quadrant, The. Bexh 7B 2
Quakers Clo. Hart 3B 28
Quantock Rd. Bexh 2D 6
Quay La. Grnh 4J 9
Quebec Rd. Til 2K 11
Queen Anne's Ga. Bexh 3G 5
Queenborough Gdns. Chst . . .6A 14
Queen Elizabeth II Bri. Dart . . .3E 8
QUEEN MARY'S HOSPITAL.
. . . . .6D 14
Queen's Farm Rd. Shorne . . .2K 23
Queens Gdns. Dart 1C 18
Queen's Rd. Eri 6J 3
Queens Rd. Grav 3B 22
Queen's Rd. Well 2D 4
Queen St. Bexh 3J 5
Queen St. Eri 6J 3
Queen St. Grav 6A 12
Queenswood Rd. Sidc 5C 4
Questor. Dart 2K 17

R

Rabbits Rd. S Dar 2E 26
Racefield Clo. Shorne 7K 23
Rackman Clo. Well 2E 4
Radfield Way. Sidc 7A 4
(in two parts)
Radley Ho. SE2 . . . . .2B 2
(off Wolvercote Rd.)
Radnor Av. Well 5E 4
Radnor Clo. Chst 6B 14
Raeburn Av. Dart 5G 7
Raeburn Pl. Swans 5B 10
Raeburn Rd. Sidc 6B 4
Raglan Rd. Belv 4D 2
Railway Pl. Belv 3E 2
Railway Pl. Grav 6A 12
Railway St. N'fleet 5D 10
Rainham Clo. SE9 . . . . .6B 4
Raleigh Clo. Eri 6K 3
Raleigh Ct. Eri 7K 3
Ramillies Rd. Sidc 6E 4
Ramsden Rd. Eri 7H 3
Randall Clo. Eri 6G 3
Randolph Clo. Bexh 3B 6
Ranelagh Gdns. N'fleet 7J 11
Range Rd. Grav 7D 12
Rangeworth Pl. Sidc 3C 14
Ranleigh Gdns. Bexh 7D 2
Ranworth Clo. Eri 2D 6
Raphael Av. Til 1K 11
Raphael Rd. Grav 7C 12
Rashleigh Way. Hort K 4D 26
Rathmore Rd. Grav 7A 12
Ravensbourne Rd. Dart 3F 7
Ravenswood. Bex 1H 15
Rayford Clo. Dart 5H 7
Ray Lamb Way. Eri 1K 3
Rayner's Ct. Grav 5E 10
Rays Hill. Hort K 4D 26
Read Way. Grav 5C 22
Rebecca Ct. Sidc 4E 14
Recreation Rd. Sidc 3B 14
Rectory Bus. Cen. Sidc 4E 14
Rectory Clo. Dart 4D 6
Rectory Clo. Sidc 4E 14
Rectory La. Sidc 4E 14
Rectory Mdw. S'fleet 6D 20
Rectory Rd. Swans 7B 10
Redding Clo. Dart 2F 19
Reddy Rd. Eri 6K 3
Redhill Rd. New Ash 4H 31
Redhill Wood. New Ash 3K 31
Red Ho. La. Bexh 4G 5
Redleaf Clo. Belv 6E 2
Red Lodge Cres. Bex 3C 16
Red Lodge Rd. Bex 3C 16
Redpoll Way. Eri 3B 2
Redstreet. 6E 20
Red St. S'fleet 5D 20
Redwood Clo. Sidc 7D 4
Redwood Ct. Dart 6B 8

Reeves Cres. Swan 3C 24
Regency Clo. W King 6B 30
Regency Way. Bexh 3G 5
Regents Ct. Grav 5A 12
Regent Sq. Belv 4F 3
Reinickendorf Av. SE9 . . . . . . .6A 4
Rembrandt Dri. N'fleet 3G 21
Rennets Clo. SE9 . . . . .5B 4
Rennets Wood Rd. SE9 . . . . . .5A 4
Renshaw Clo. Belv 6D 2
Reservoir Clo. Grnh 6K 9
Restons Cres. SE9 . . . . .6A 4
Ribblesdale Rd. Dart 1D 18
Ricardo Path. SE28 . . . . .1A 2
Richardson Clo. Grnh 5G 9
Richmer Rd. Eri 2J 3
Richmond Dri. Grav 2D 22
Rider Clo. Sidc 6B 4
Ridge Av. Dart 6E 6
Ridgecroft Clo. Bex 1B 16
Ridge, The. Bex 7J 5
Ridge Way. Cray 6E 6
Ridgeway. Dart 5F 19
Ridgeway Av. Grav 3A 22
Ridgeway Bungalows.
Shorne 7K 23
Ridgeway E. Sidc 5C 4
Ridgeway, The. Shorne 7K 23
Ridgeway W. Sidc 5B 4
Ridgewood. Long 2F 29
Ridley. 5K 31
Ridley Rd. Well 1E 4
Riefield Rd. SE9 . . . . .4A 4
Ripley Rd. Belv 4E 2
Ripleys Mkt. Dart 7K 7
Rippersley Rd. Well 1D 4
Risedale Rd. Bexh 3B 6
Rise, The. Bex 7F 5
Rise, The. Dart 7J 5
Rise, The. Grav 4D 22
Riverdale Rd. Bex 7J 5
Riverdale Rd. Eri 5F 3
Riversdale. N'fleet 3H 21
Riverside Ind. Est. Dart 5K 7
Riverside Rail Freight Terminal.
Til 4K 11
Riverside Rd. Sidc 3H 15
Riverside Way. Dart 5K 7
Riverview. Dart 4B 8
(off Henderson Dri.)
Riverview Park. 4E 22
Riverview Rd. Grnh 5H 9
River Wharf Bus. Pk. Belv 1H 3
Roberts Clo. SE9 . . . . .1A 14
Roberts Rd. Belv 5E 2
Robina Av. Grav 7G 11
Robina Clo. Bexh 4G 5
Robina Ct. Swan 4F 25
Robin Hood La. Bexh 5H 5
Robyns Cft. N'fleet 4H 21
Rochester Clo. Sidc 6E 4
Rochester Dri. Bex 6J 5
Rochester Rd. Dart 7B 8
Rochester Rd. Grav 7D 12
Rochester Way. SE3 & SE9 . . .3A 4
Rochester Way. Dart 7C 6
Rodeo Clo. Eri 1G 7
Roehampton Clo. Grav 7D 12
Roehampton Dri. Chst 6A 14
Rogers Ct. Swan 4F 25
Rogers Wood La. Fawk 4D 30
Rokesby Clo. Well 2A 4
Rollo Rd. Swan 7E 16
Roman Rd. N'fleet 3F 21
Roman Villa Rd. Dart 5D 18
Roman Way. Dart 5D 6
Romney Gdns. Bexh 1J 5
Romney Rd. N'fleet 3H 21
Ronaldstone Rd. Sidc 6B 4
Rondel Ct. Bex 6H 5
Roseacre Rd. Well 3E 4
Rose Av. Grav 1D 22
Rosebank Gdns. N'fleet 1H 21
Roseberry Gdns. Dart 7H 7
Rosebery Av. Sidc 1A 14
Rosebery Ct. N'fleet 1J 21
Rosedale Clo. Dart 7C 8

Rosedene Ct. Dart 7H 7
Rosegarth. 1st R 1H 29
Rosemary Rd. Well 1C 4
Rose St. N'fleet 6E 10
Rose Vs. Dart 7C 8
Rosewood. Dart 4D 16
Rosewood Clo. Sidc 3F 15
Rosher Ho. Grav 6J 11
Rosherville. 6H 11
Rosherville Way. Grav 7H 11
Rossland Clo. Bexh 5A 6
Ross Rd. Dart 6F 7
Rouge La. Grav 1A 22
Round Ash Way. Hart 6B 28
Rowan Clo. Meop 6K 29
Rowan Cres. Dart 1H 17
Rowan Ho. Sidc 3C 14
Rowan Rd. Bexh 3H 5
Rowan Rd. Swan 3C 24
Rowans Clo. Long 2A 28
Rowanwood Av. Sidc 1D 14
Rowhill Rd. Swan & Dart 6E 16
Rowlatt Clo. Dart 4H 17
Rowlatt Rd. Dart 4H 17
Rowley Av. Sidc 7E 4
Rownmarsh Clo. N'fleet 3G 21
Rowntree Path. SE28 . . . . . . .1A 2
Row, The. New Ash 2J 31
Rowzill Rd. Swan 6E 16
Royal Oak Rd. Bexh 5J 5
(in two parts)
Royal Oak Ter. Grav 1B 22
(off Constitution Hill)
Royal Pde. Chst 7A 14
Royal Pde. M. Chst 7A 14
(off Royal Pde.)
Royal Pier M. Grav 6B 12
Royal Pier Rd. Grav 6A 12
Royal Rd. Dart 5B 18
Royal Rd. Sidc 3G 15
Royston Rd. Dart 6E 6
Rudland Rd. Bexh 3A 6
Ruffets Wood. Grav 6B 22
Rumania Wlk. Grav 3E 22
Runnymede Ct. Dart 1D 18
Rural Va. N'fleet 7H 11
Rushdene. SE2 . . . . .3A 2
(in two parts)
Rushetts Rd. W King 7B 30
Ruskin Av. Well 2D 4
Ruskin Dri. Well 3D 4
Ruskin Gro. Dart 5B 8
Ruskin Gro. Well 2D 4
Ruskin Rd. Belv 4E 2
Russell Clo. Bexh 4K 5
Russell Clo. Dart 4F 7
Russell Pl. S at H 1B 26
Russell Rd. Grav 6C 12
Russell Rd. Til 1H 11
Russell Sq. Long 3A 28
Russell Ter. Hort K 4D 26
Russets, The. Meop 6K 29
Russett Way. Swan 2C 24
Rutland Av. Sidc 7D 4
Rutland Clo. Bex 2G 15
Rutland Clo. Dart 7J 7
Rutland Ct. SE9 . . . . .2A 14
Rutland Ga. Belv 5F 3
Ruxley. 6G 15
Ruxley Clo. Sidc 6G 15
Ruxley Corner Ind. Est.
Sidc 6G 15
Ruxton Clo. Swan 3D 24
Ruxton Ct. Swan 3D 24
Rydal Dri. Bexh 1K 5
Rye Clo. Bex 6A 6
Ryecroft. Grav 5D 22
Ryecroft. Long H 4G 29

S

Sackville Rd. Dart 2J 17
Saddington St. Grav 7A 12
St Aidan's Way. Grav 3D 22
St Alban's Clo. Grav 3C 22
St Alban's Gdns. Grav 3C 22

St Alban's Rd. Dart 7A 8
St Andrew's Ct. Grav 6A 12
(off Queen St.)
St Andrews Ct. Swan 3D 24
St Andrew's Rd. Grav 7A 12
St Andrew's Rd. Sidc 3G 15
St Andrew's Rd. Til 1H 11
St Audrey Av. Bexh 2K 5
St Augustine's Rd. Belv 4D 2
St Benedict's Av. Grav 2C 22
St Botolph Rd. Grav 3G 21
St Brides Clo. Eri 2B 2
St Chad's Dri. Grav 3D 22
St Chads Rd. Til 2K 11
St Clement's Clo. N'fleet 3J 21
St Clements Way. Grnh 5H 9
St Columba's Clo. Grav 3C 22
(in two parts)
St David's Cres. Grav 4C 22
St Davids Rd. Swan 6E 16
St Dunstan's Dri. Grav 4D 22
St Edmunds Clo. Eri 2B 2
St Edmund's Rd. Dart 4A 8
St Fidelis Rd. Eri 4H 3
St Francis Av. Grav 4D 22
St Francis Rd. Eri 4H 3
St George's Cres. Grav 4C 22
St George's Rd. Sidc 6G 15
St George's Rd. Swan 4E 24
St George's Shop. Cen.
Grav 6A 12
St Georges Sq. Grav 6A 12
St Georges Sq. Long 3B 28
St Gregory's Ct. Grav 2D 22
St Gregory's Cres. Grav 2D 22
St Helen's Rd. Eri 2B 2
St Hilda's Way. Grav 4C 22
St James Ct. Grnh 6F 9
St James La. Grnh 1F 19
St James Oak. Grav 7K 11
St James Pl. Dart 6J 7
St James's Av. Grav 7K 11
St James Sq. Long 3B 28
St James's Rd. Grav 6K 11
St James's St. Grav 6K 11
St James Way. Sidc 5H 15
St John Fisher Rd. Eri 3B 2
St John's Clo. Hart 5C 28
St John's Ct. Eri 4H 3
St John's Jerusalem Garden.
. . . . .7C 18
St John's La. Hart 6C 28
St Johns Pde. Sidc 4D 14
(off Sidcup High St.)
St John's Rd. Dart 7D 8
St John's Rd. Eri 5H 3
St John's Rd. Grav 7C 12
St John's Rd. Sidc 4E 14
St John's Rd. Well 3E 4
St Katherine's Rd. Eri 2B 2
St Leonard's Clo. Well 3D 4
St Luke's Clo. Dart 5F 19
St Luke's Clo. Swan 2C 24
St Margarets. 7F 19
St Margaret's Av. Sidc 3A 14
St Margaret's Clo. Dart 2E 18
St Margaret's Cres. Grav 3D 22
St Margaret's Rd. N'fleet 1H 21
St Margarets Rd.
S Dar & Grn St 7F 19
St Mark's Av. N'fleet 7H 11
St Martin's Clo. Eri 2B 2
St Martin's Rd. Dart 6A 8
St Mary's Clo. Grav 2B 22
St Mary's Rd. Bex 1B 16
St Mary's Rd. Grnh 5F 9
St Mary's Rd. Swan 4C 24
St Mary's Way. Long 3B 28
St Michael's Clo. Eri 2B 2
St Michael's Ri. Well 1E 4
St Michael's Rd. Well 3E 4
St Patrick's Gdns. Grav 3C 22
St Paul's Clo. Swans 7B 10
St Paul's Cray Rd. Chst 7A 14
St Paul's Rd. Eri 7G 3
St Paul's Wood Hill. Orp 7D 14
St Peter's Clo. Chst 7A 14

St Peter's Clo. *Swans* 7C **10**
St Quentin Rd. *Well* 3C **4**
St Saviours Wlk. *Dart* 6K **7**
(off Bullace La.)
St Thomas' Almshouses.
Grav 1K **21**
St Thomas Ct. *Bex* 7K **5**
St Thomas Rd. *Belv* 2G **3**
St Thomas Rd. *N'fleet* 2H **21**
St Thomas's Av. *Grav* 1A **22**
St Vincents Dart 5B **8**
St Vincents Rd. *Dart* 6B **8**
St Vincents Vs. *Dart* 6A **8**
Salcote Rd. *Grav* 5D **22**
Salem Pl. *N'fleet* 7G **11**
Salisbury Av. *Swan* 4F **25**
Salisbury Rd. *Bex* 1K **15**
Salisbury Rd. *Dart* 7D **8**
Salisbury Rd. *Grav* 1J **21**
Salmon Rd. *Belv* 5E **2**
Salmon Rd. *Dart* 3A **8**
Saltash Rd. *Well* 1F **5**
Saltcote Clo. *Dart* 6D **6**
Saltford Clo. *Eri* 5J **3**
Sampson Clo. *Belv* 3B **2**
Sanctuary Clo. *Dart* 6H **7**
Sanctuary, The. *Bex* 6G **5**
Sandalwood Ho. *Sidc* 3C **14**
Sandbanks Hill. *Bean* 6J **19**
Sandcliff Rd. *Eri* 4H **3**
Sanderling Ct. *SE28* 1A **2**
Sanderling Way. *Grnh* 5H **9**
Sandford Rd. *Bexh* 4H **5**
Sandgate Rd. *Well* 7A **2**
Sandhurst Rd. *Bex* 5G **5**
Sandhurst Rd. *Sidc* 3C **14**
Sandhurst Rd. *Til* 2B **12**
Sandown Rd. *Grav* 6B **22**
Sandpiper Clo. *Grnh* 6H **9**
Sandpiper Dri. *Eri* 2K **3**
Sandpipers, The. *Grav* 2C **22**
Sandpit Rd. *Dart* 4H **7**
Sandringham Ct. *Sidc* 6C **4**
Sandringham Dri. *Bex* 2D **16**
Sandringham Dri. *Well* 2B **4**
Sandy Bank Rd. *Grav* 1A **22**
Sandy La. *Bean* 2K **19**
(in two parts)
Sandy La. *St P & Sidc* 7G **15**
Sapho Pk. *Grav* 4E **22**
Sara Cres. *Grnh* 4J **9**
Sara Ho. *Eri* 7J **3**
Sara Pk. *Grav* 4D **22**
Saunders Clo. *N'fleet* 2H **21**
Saunders Way. *Dart* 2A **18**
Savoy Rd. *Dart* 5J **7**
Saxon Clo. *N'fleet* 3F **21**
Saxon Pl. *Hort K* 5D **26**
Saxon Rd. *Dart* 4K **17**
Saxon Wlk. *Sidc* 6F **15**
Sayer Rd. *Grnh* 5H **9**
School Clo. *Meop* 7K **29**
School Cres. *Cray* 4E **6**
School La. *Bean* 4K **19**
School La. *Hort K* 4D **26**
School La. *Swan* 1G **25**
School La. *Well* 3E **4**
School Rd. *Grav* 3B **22**
(in two parts)
Schooner Ct. *Dart* 4D **8**
Scott Cres. *Eri* 1E **6**
Scott Ho. *Belv* 5D **2**
Scott Rd. *Grav* 5C **22**
Scratchers La. *Fawk* 3A **30**
Scudders Hill. *Fawk* 6J **27**
Seacourt Rd. *SE2* 2B **2**
Seaton Rd. *Dart* 7F **7**
Seaton Rd. *Well* 7A **2**
Sedcombe Clo. *Sidc* 4E **14**
Sedgemere Rd. *SE2* 3A **2**
Sedley. *S'fleet* 6D **20**
Selah Dri. *Swan* 1B **24**
Selborne Av. *Bex* 1H **15**
Selborne Rd. *Sidc* 4E **14**
Selbourne Clo. *Long* 3G **29**
Selkirk Dri. *Eri* 1D **6**
Selsey Cres. *Well* 1G **5**

Selwyn Cres. *Well* 3E **4**
Selwyn Rd. *Til* 2J **11**
Sermon Dri. *Swan* 3B **24**
Seven Acres. *New Ash* 3H **31**
Seven Acres. *Swan* 6C **24**
Sevenoaks Clo. *Bexh* 4A **6**
Sevenoaks Way. *Sidc* 7F **15**
Sewell Rd. *SE2* 2A **2**
Sexton Rd. *Til* 1J **11**
Seymour Rd. *N'fleet* 1J **21**
Seymour Rd. *Til* 1J **11**
Seymour Wlk. *Swans* 7B **10**
Shaftesbury La. *Dart* 4C **8**
Shaftesbury Ct. *Eri* 1E **6**
(off Selkirk Dri.)
Shakespeare Av. *Til* 2A **12**
Shakespeare Rd. *Bexh* 1H **5**
Shakespeare Rd. *Dart* 4B **8**
Shamrock Rd. *Grav* 7D **12**
Sharland Rd. *Grav* 2B **22**
Sharman Ct. *Sidc* 4D **14**
(off Carlton Rd.)
Sharnbrooke Clo. *Well* 3F **5**
Sharp Way. *Dart* 3A **8**
Shaw Clo. *SE28* 1A **2**
Shaw Cres. *Til* 1A **12**
Shaw Ho. *Belv* 5D **2**
Shears Clo. *Dart* 2H **17**
Shears Grn. Ct. *Grav* 2K **21**
Shearwater. *Long* 3E **28**
Shearwood Cres. *Dart* 3E **6**
Shelbury Clo. *Sidc* 3D **14**
Sheldon Rd. *Bexh* 1J **5**
Shellbank La.
Bean & G Str 6H **19**
Shelley Dri. *Well* 1B **4**
Shelley Pl. *Til* 1A **12**
Shenley Rd. *Dart* 6B **8**
Shenstone Clo. *Dart* 4C **6**
Shepherds Grn. *Chst* 7A **14**
Shepherd's La. *Dart* 1F **17**
Shepherds Leas. *SE9* 4A **4**
Shepherd St. *N'fleet* 7G **11**
Sheppey Clo. *Eri* 2K **3**
Sheppy Pl. *Grav* 7A **12**
Sherbourne Clo. *W King* 6B **30**
Sherbrooke Clo. *Bexh* 4K **5**
Sheridan Clo. *Swan* 4E **24**
Sheridan Ct. *Dart* 4B **8**
Sheridan Rd. *Belv* 4E **2**
Sheridan Rd. *Bexh* 3H **5**
Shermanbury Pl. *Eri* 7K **3**
Sherwood Clo. *Bex* 6F **5**
Sherwood Pk. Av. *Sidc* 7D **4**
Sherwood Rd. *Well* 2B **4**
Shieldhall St. *SE2* 4A **2**
Shinglewell Rd. *Eri* 7E **2**
Ship La. *S at H* 1J **25**
Shire Ct. *Eri* 3B **2**
Shirehall Rd. *Dart* 5H **17**
Shirley Av. *Bex* 7G **5**
Shirley Clo. *Dart* 4H **7**
Shirley Clo. *Grav* 1G **23**
Shirley Rd. *Sidc* 3B **14**
Shooters Hill. *SE18 & Well* . . .3A **4**
Shoreham Clo. *Bex* 1G **15**
Shore, The. *N'fleet* 5F **11**
(in two parts)
Shorne. 5K **23**
Shorne Clo. *Sidc* 6E **4**
Shorne Ifield Rd. *Shorne* 6F **23**
Shornells Way. *SE2* 4A **2**
Shorne Ridgeway. 7K **23**
Shorne Wood Country Pk. . .7G **23**
Shorne Wood Country Pk.
Vis. Cen. 7H **23**
Shortlands Clo. *Belv* 3D **2**
Shrimp Brand Cotts. *Grav* . . .5K **21**
Shrubbery Rd. *Grav* 1A **22**
Shrubbery Rd. *S Dar* 1E **26**
Shurlock Av. *Swan* 2C **24**
Shuttle Clo. *Sidc* 7C **4**
Shuttlemead. *Bex* 7J **5**
Shuttle Rd. *Dart* 3F **7**
Sibley Clo. *Bexh* 5H **5**
Sidcup. 4D **14**
Sidcup By-Pass. *Chst* 3A **14**

Sidcup High St. *Sidc* 4D **14**
Sidcup Hill. *Sidc* 4E **14**
Sidcup Hill Gdns. *Sidc* 5F **15**
Sidcup Pl. *Sidc* 5D **14**
Sidcup Rd. *SE12 & SE9* 3A **14**
Sidcup Technical Cen.
Sidc 6G **15**
Sidewood Rd. *SE9* 1A **14**
Sidings, The. *Meop* 5K **29**
Sidmouth Ct. *Dart* 1C **18**
(off Churchill Clo.)
Sidmouth Rd. *Well* 7A **2**
Silecroft Rd. *Bexh* 1K **5**
Silver Birch Clo. *Dart* 4D **16**
Silverdale. *Hart* 4C **28**
Silverdale Rd. *Bexh* 2A **6**
Silver Rd. *Grav* 2D **22**
Silver Spring Clo. *Eri* 6F **3**
Simmonds Dri. *Hart* 5D **28**
Sinclair Way. *Dart* 4E **18**
Singlewell. 5B **22**
Singlewell Rd. *Grav* 1A **22**
(in two parts)
Sirdar Strand. *Grav* 5E **22**
Skinney La. *Hort K* 3E **26**
Skippers Clo. *Grnh* 5J **9**
Slade Gdns. *Eri* 1E **6**
Slade Green. 1F **7**
Slade Grn. Rd. *Eri* 2K **3**
Slades Dri. *Chst* 4A **14**
Sloane Sq. *Long* 3B **28**
Slocum Clo. *SE28* 1A **2**
Small Grains. *Fawk* 3E **30**
Smarden Clo. *Belv* 5E **2**
Smarts Rd. *Grav* 3A **22**
Smugglers Wlk. *Grnh* 5J **9**
Smythe Rd. *S at H* 1B **26**
Snelling Av. *N'fleet* 2H **21**
Snipe Clo. *Eri* 2K **3**
Somerhill Av. *Sidc* 7E **4**
Somerhill Rd. *Well* 3E **4**
Somerset Av. *Well* 5C **4**
Somerset Rd. *Dart* 6G **7**
Somersham Rd. *Bexh* 2H **5**
Somerville Rd. *Dart* 6A **8**
Sorrel Way. *N'fleet* 4H **21**
Sounds Lodge. *Swan* 6B **24**
S. Ash Rd. *Ash* 7G **31**
South Clo. *Bexh* 4G **5**
South Darenth. 1D **26**
Southern Pl. *Swan* 4C **24**
Southey Wlk. *Til* 1A **12**
Southfields. *Swan* 7D **16**
Southfields Rd. *W King* 7C **30**
Southfleet. 5D **20**
Southfleet Av. *Long* 2E **28**
Southfleet Rd. *Bean* 4K **19**
Southfleet Rd. *N'fleet* 1J **21**
Southfleet Rd. *Swans* 7C **10**
S. Gipsy Rd. *Well* 3G **5**
S. Glade, The. *Bex* 1J **15**
S. Hall Clo. *F'ham* 7A **26**
S. Hill Rd. *Grav* 1B **22**
S. Kent Av. *N'fleet* 6F **11**
South Rd. *Eri* 7K **3**
South Side. *Til* 4H **11**
Southspring. *Sidc* 7A **4**
South St. *Grav* 7A **12**
South Ter. *F'ham* 7A **26**
S. View Av. *Til* 1K **11**
S. View Clo. *Bex* 6J **5**
S. View Clo. *Swan* 4F **25**
S. View Rd. *Dart* 3J **17**
Southwold Rd. *Bex* 6A **6**
Sovereign Ct. S at H 1C **26**
(off Ship La.)
Sparepenny La.
Eyns & F'ham 7K **25**
Sparrows La. *SE9* 1A **14**
Speedgate Hill. *Fawk* 2D **30**
Spencer St. *Grav* 7K **11**
Spencer Wlk. *Til* 2K **11**
Spielman Rd. *Dart* 4A **8**
Spindles. *Til* 1K **11**
Spinney, The. *Sidc* 5H **15**
Spinney, The. *Swan* 2D **24**

Spire Clo. *Grav* 1A **22**
Spires, The. *Dart* 2J **17**
Spital St. *Dart* 6J **7**
Springcroft. *Hart* 6D **28**
Spring Cross. *New Ash* 3K **31**
Springfield Av. *Swan* 4E **24**
Springfield Rd. *Bexh* 3A **6**
Springfield Rd. *Well* 3E **4**
Spring Gro. *Grav* 1A **22**
Springhead Enterprise Pk.
N'fleet 1E **20**
Springhead Rd. *Eri* 6K **3**
Springhead Rd. *N'fleet* 2F **21**
Spring Va. *Bexh* 4A **6**
Spring Va. *Grnh* 6K **9**
Spring Va. Clo. *Swan* 1E **24**
Springvale Ct. *N'fleet* 2F **21**
Spring Va. N. *Dart* 7J **7**
Spring Va. S. *Dart* 7J **7**
Sprucedale Clo. *Swan* 2D **24**
Spurrell Av. *Bex* 4C **16**
Square, The. *Swan* 3C **24**
Squires Fld. *Hex* 1F **25**
Squires Way. *Dart* 4C **16**
Stacey Clo. *Grav* 5D **22**
Stacklands Clo. *W King* 6B **30**
Stack La. *Hart* 5B **28**
Stack Rd. *Hort K* 4E **26**
Stadium Way. *Dart* 5D **6**
Stafford Clo. *Grnh* 5G **9**
Stafford Rd. *Sidc* 4B **14**
Staines Wlk. *Sidc* 6F **15**
Stainmore Clo. *Chst* 7A **14**
Stanbrook Rd. *Grav* 1J **21**
Standard Rd. *Belv* 5E **2**
Standard Rd. *Bexh* 4H **5**
Stanham Pl. *Dart* 4F **7**
Stanham Rd. *Dart* 5H **7**
Stanhill Cotts. *Dart* 7C **16**
Stanhope Rd. *Bexh* 2H **5**
Stanhope Rd. *Sidc* 4D **14**
Stanhope Rd. *Swans* 6C **10**
Stanley Clo. *Grnh* 5F **9**
Stanley Cotts. *Grn St* 5F **19**
Stanley Cres. *Grav* 5C **22**
Stanley Rd. *N'fleet* 2H **21**
Stanley Rd. *Sidc* 3D **14**
Stanley Rd. *Swans* 6C **10**
Stanmore Rd. *Belv* 4G **3**
Stansted Cres. *Bex* 1G **15**
Staple Clo. *Bex* 3C **16**
Staples, The. *Swan* 1G **25**
Stapleton Rd. *Bexh* 7D **2**
Stapley Rd. *Belv* 5E **2**
Starboard Av. *Grnh* 6J **9**
Star Hill. *Dart* 5D **6**
Starling Clo. *Long* 3E **28**
Station App. *B'hurst* 2B **6**
Station App. *Bex* 1K **15**
Station App. *Bexh* 2H **5**
Station App. *Cray* 6E **6**
Station App. *Dart* 6K **7**
Station App. *Meop* 5K **29**
Station App. *Swan* 4D **24**
Station App. *Well* 2D **4**
(in three parts)
Station App. N. *Sidc* 2D **14**
Station Pde. *Bexh* 2H **5**
(off Pickford La.)
Station Pde. *Eri* 5J **3**
Station Pde. *Sidc* 2D **14**
Station Rd. *Belv* 3E **2**
Station Rd. *Bexh* 3H **5**
Station Rd. *Cray* 7E **6**
Station Rd. *Grnh* 5H **9**
(in two parts)
Station Rd. *Long* 3B **28**
Station Rd. *Meop* 5K **29**
Station Rd. *N'fleet* 6E **10**
Station Rd. *Sidc* 2D **14**
Station Rd. *S Dar* 2C **26**
Station Rd. *S'fleet* 4C **20**
Station Rd. *Swan* 4D **24**
Station Rd. N. *Belv* 3F **3**
Stedman Clo. *Bex* 3D **16**
Steele Av. *Grnh* 5G **9**
Steele Wlk. *Eri* 7F **3**

Stelling Rd.—Upton Rd. S.

Stelling Rd. *Eri* 7H **3**
Stephen Rd. *Bexh* 3B **6**
Stephenson Av. *Til* 1K **11**
Sterndale Rd. *Dart* 7A **8**
Stevannie Ct. *Belv* 5E **2**
Stevedale Rd. *Well* 2F **5**
Stevens Clo. *Bex* 4C **16**
Stevens Clo. *Dart* 5F **19**
Stevenson Clo. *Eri* 2K **3**
Steynton Av. *Bex* 2G **15**
Stickland Rd. *Belv* 4E **2**
Stiles Clo. *Eri* 5F **3**
Stock La. *Dart* 3H **17**
Stokesay Ct. Dart *6C* ***8***
(off Osbourne Rd.)
Stone **5F 9**
Stonebridge Rd. *N'fleet* 5D **10**
Stone Ct. *Eri* 5K **3**
Stonecroft Rd. *Eri* 7G **3**
Stonefield Clo. *Bexh* 3K **5**
Stonehill Green **7B 16**
Stonehill Woods Pk. *Sidc* 6A **16**
STONE HOUSE HOSPITAL 6D **8**
Stone Pl. Rd. *Grnh* 5F **9**
Stones Cross Rd. *Swan* 5B **24**
Stone St. *Grav* 6A **12**
Stonewood **3K 19**
Stonewood. *Bean* 3K **19**
Stonewood Rd. *Eri* 5J **3**
Stony Corner. *Grav* 4H **29**
Stornaway Strand. *Grav* 3E **22**
Stour Rd. *Dart* 3F **7**
Stow Ct. *Dart* 7D **8**
Strand Clo. *Meop* 7K **29**
Stratton Clo. *Bexh* 3H **5**
Stratton Rd. *Bexh* 3H **5**
Strawberry Fields. *Swan* 1D **24**
Stream Way. *Belv* 6D **2**
Street, The. *Ash* 5G **31**
Street, The. *Hort K* 4C **26**
Street, The. *Shorne* 5K **23**
Strickland Av. *Dart* 3A **8**
(in two parts)
Struttons Av. *N'fleet* 2J **21**
Stuart Clo. *Swan* 7E **16**
Stuart Evans Clo. *Well* 3F **5**
Stuart Mantle Way. *Eri* 7J **3**
Stuart Rd. *Grav* 6K **11**
Stuart Rd. *Well* 1E **4**
Studios, The. New Ash *2J* ***31***
(off Row, The)
Studland Clo. *Sidc* 3C **14**
Studley Ct. *Sidc* 5E **14**
Studley Cres. *Long* 2F **29**
Sturges Fld. *Chst* 6A **14**
Suffolk Rd. *Dart* 6K **7**
(in two parts)
Suffolk Rd. *Grav* 6C **12**
Suffolk Rd. *Sidc* 6F **15**
Sullivan Clo. *Dart* 6G **7**
Sullivan Rd. *Til* 1K **11**
Summerhill Rd. *Dart* 7J **7**
Summerhouse Dri.
Bex & Dart 4C **16**
Sun Ct. *Eri* 2E **6**
Sundridge Av. *Well* 2A **4**
Sundridge Clo. *Dart* 6B **8**
Sun Hill. *Fawk* 3D **30**
Sunland Av. *Bexh* 4H **5**
Sun La. *Grav* 2B **22**
Sunninghill. *N'fleet* 2H **21**
Sun Rd. *Swans* 6C **10**
Sunset Clo. *Eri* 2K **3**
Surrey Clo. *W King* 7B **30**
Sussex Clo. *W King* 7B **30**
Sussex Pl. *Eri* 7F **3**
Sussex Rd. *Dart* 7B **8**
Sussex Rd. *Eri* 7F **3**
Sussex Rd. *Sidc* 5E **14**
Sutcliffe Rd. *Well* 2F **5**
Sutherland Av. *Well* 4B **4**
Sutherland Clo. *Grav* 2G **23**
Sutherland Clo. *Grnh* 5G **9**
Sutherland Rd. *Belv* 3E **2**
Sutton at Hone **7C 18**
Swaisland Dri. *Cray* 5E **6**
Swaisland Rd. *Dart* 5G **7**
Swalecliffe Rd. *Belv* 5F **3**
Swaledale Rd. *Dart* 1D **18**
Swale Rd. *Dart* 4F **7**
Swallow Clo. *Eri* 1D **6**
Swallow Clo. *Grnh* 5G **9**
Swallowfields. *N'fleet* 3H **21**
Swanbridge Rd. *Bexh* 1K **5**
Swan Bus. Pk. *Dart* 4J **7**
Swan La. *Dart* 7E **6**
Swanley **4E 24**
Swanley By-Pass.
Sidc & Swan 1A **24**
Swanley Cen. *Swan* 3D **24**
Swanley Interchange.
(Junct.) **6G 25**
Swanley La. *Swan* 3E **24**
Swanley Rd. *Well* 1F **5**
Swanley Village **1G 25**
Swanley Village Rd. *Swan* 1G **25**
Swanscombe **5C 10**
Swanscombe Bus. Cen.
Swans 4B **10**
Swanscombe St. *Swans* 7B **10**
Swanton Rd. *Eri* 7E **2**
Swaylands Rd. *Belv* 6E **2**
Sweyne Rd. *Swans* 6B **10**
Swiller's La. *Shorne* 5K **23**
(in two parts)
Swinburne Gdns. *Til* 2A **12**
Swingate La. *SE18* 1B **4**
Sycamore Av. *Sidc* 6C **4**
Sycamore Clo. *Grav* 7C **12**
Sycamore Clo. *Til* 2K **11**
Sycamore Ct. Eri *5H* ***3***
(off Sandcliff Rd.)
Sycamore Ct. *Grnh* 7F **9**
Sycamore Dri. *Swan* 3D **24**
Sycamore M. Eri *5H* ***3***
(off St John's Rd.)
Sycamore Rd. *Dart* 1J **17**
Sydney Rd. *SE2* 3A **2**
Sydney Rd. *Bexh* 4G **5**
Sydney Rd. *Sidc* 4B **14**
Sydney Rd. *Til* 2K **11**
Symonds Clo. *W King* 5B **30**

T

Tallents Clo. *S at H* 7C **18**
Tamesis Strand. *Grav* 5D **22**
Tanhurst Wlk. *SE2* 3B **2**
Tanyard Cotts. *Shorne* 6K **23**
Tanyard Hill. *Shorne* 6K **23**
Tanyard La. *Bex* 7K **5**
Tarling Clo. *Sidc* 3E **14**
Tates Orchard. *Long* 6C **28**
Taunton Clo. *Bexh* 2C **6**
Taunton Rd. *N'fleet* 5D **10**
Taunton Va. *Grav* 3C **22**
Tavistock Rd. *Well* 1F **5**
Tavy Bri. *SE2* 2A **2**
Tavy Bri. Cen. *SE2* 2A **2**
Taylor Row. *Dart* 3H **17**
Taylors Clo. *Sidc* 3C **14**
Teardrop Ind. Est. *Swan* 5G **25**
Teesdale Rd. *Dart* 1D **18**
Teeswater Ct. *Eri* 3B **2**
Teignmouth Rd. *Well* 2F **5**
Telford Rd. *SE9* 2A **14**
Templar Dri. *Grav* 5K **21**
Templars Ct. *Dart* 5B **8**
Temple Hill **5A 8**
Temple Hill. *Dart* 6A **8**
Temple Hill Sq. *Dart* 5A **8**
Tenby Rd. *Well* 1G **5**
Tennants Row. *Til* 2H **11**
Tennyson Clo. *Well* 1B **4**
Tennyson Ho. *Belv* 5D **2**
Tennyson Rd. *Dart* 5B **8**
Tennyson Wlk. *N'fleet* 3G **21**
Tennyson Wlk. *Til* 2A **12**
Tensing Av. *N'fleet* 3H **21**
Terence Clo. *Grav* 1E **22**
Terence Ct. Belv *6D* ***2***
(off Charton Clo.)
Terraces, The. *Dart* 7D **8**
Terrace St. *Grav* 6A **12**
(in two parts)
Terrace, The. *Grav* 6A **12**
(in three parts)
Teviot Clo. *Well* 1E **4**
Thackeray Av. *Til* 1A **12**
Thames Ga. *Dart* 5B **8**
Thameside Aviation Mus.
1J **13**
Thamesmead **1A 2**
Thamesmead East **2E 2**
Thamesmead South **2B 2**
Thames Rd. *Cray* 2E **6**
Thames Way. *Grav* 1G **21**
(in two parts)
Thanet Ho. *Grav* 1J **21**
Thanet Rd. *Bex* 7K **5**
Thanet Rd. *Eri* 7J **3**
Thatcher Ct. *Dart* 7J **7**
Thelma Clo. *Grav* 5E **22**
Third Av. *N'fleet* 1H **21**
Thirlmere Rd. *Bexh* 2B **6**
Thirza Rd. *Dart* 6A **8**
Thistlebrook. *SE2* 2A **2**
Thistle Ct. Dart *1C* ***18***
(off Churchill Clo.)
Thistledown. *Grav* 6C **22**
Thistlefield Clo. *Bex* 1G **15**
Thistle Rd. *Grav* 7D **12**
Thomas Dri. *Grav* 2C **22**
Thong **6F 23**
Thong La. *Grav & Shorne* 4E **22**
Thorne Clo. *Eri* 6F **3**
Thornton Rd. *Belv* 4F **3**
Three Corners. *Bexh* 2A **6**
Three Gates Rd. *Fawk* 3C **30**
Thrift, The. *Bean* 3K **19**
Throwley Clo. *SE2* 3A **2**
(in two parts)
Thurrock Pk. Way. *Til* 1G **11**
Thursland Rd. *Sidc* 5H **15**
Thwaite Clo. *Eri* 6G **3**
Ticehurst Clo. *Orp* 7D **14**
Tickford Clo. *SE2* 2A **2**
Tidford Rd. *Well* 2C **4**
Tilbury **2K 11**
Tilbury Fort **4B 12**
Tilehurst Point. *SE2* 2B **2**
Tile Kiln La. *Bex* 2B **16**
(in two parts)
Till Av. *F'ham* 7A **26**
Tillet Pl. *Til* 1A **12**
Tilmans Mead. *F'ham* 7A **26**
Timothy Clo. *Bexh* 5H **5**
Timothy Ho. Eri *2C* ***2***
(off Kale Rd.)
Titmuss Av. *SE28* 1A **2**
Tivoli Gdns. *Grav* 1A **22**
Tolcairn Ct. *Belv* 5E **2**
Tollgate Rd. *Dart* 7E **8**
Tooley St. *N'fleet* 7G **11**
Top Dartford Rd.
Swan & Dart 7E **16**
Torbrook Clo. *Bex* 6H **5**
Toronto Rd. *Til* 2K **11**
Torrens Wlk. *Grav* 5D **22**
Tor Rd. *Well* 1F **5**
Totnes Rd. *Well* 7A **2**
Tourist Info. Cen. **6B 6**
(Bexley)
Tourist Info. Cen. **4K 5**
(Bexleyheath)
Tourist Info. Cen. **7A 12**
(Gravesend)
Tourist Info. Cen. **3D 24**
(Swanley)
Tower Clo. *Grav* 5D **22**
Tower Pk. Rd. *Cray* 5E **6**
Tower Retail Pk. *Dart* 5E **6**
Tower Rd. *Belv* 4G **3**
Tower Rd. *Bexh* 4K **5**
Tower Rd. *Dart* 6H **7**
Towers Wood. *S Dar* 1E **26**
Townfield Corner. *Grav* 1B **22**
Townley Rd. *Bexh* 5J **5**
Townshend Clo. *Sidc* 6E **14**
Town Sq. *Eri* 6J **3**
Tradescant Dri. *Meop* 6K **29**
Trafalgar Ct. Eri *7K* ***3***
(off Frobisher Rd.)
Trafalgar Rd. *Dart* 2K **17**
Trafalgar Rd. *Grav* 7K **11**
Tranquil Ri. *Eri* 5J **3**
Trebble Rd. *Swans* 6B **10**
Tredegar Rd. *Dart* 2F **17**
Treetops. *Grav* 5A **22**
Treetops Clo. *SE2* 5C **2**
Trefoil Ho. Eri *2C* ***2***
(off Kale Rd.)
Trevelyan Clo. *Dart* 4A **8**
Trevithick Dri. *Dart* 4A **8**
Trewsbury Ho. *SE2* 1B **2**
Triangle, The. Sidc *7D* ***4***
(off Burnt Oak La.)
Trinity Ct. Dart *1C* ***18***
(off Churchill Clo.)
Trinity Gdns. *Dart* 6J **7**
Trinity Pl. *Bexh* 4J **5**
Trinity Rd. *Grav* 7B **12**
Trivett Clo. *Grnh* 5H **9**
Trosley Av. *Grav* 2A **22**
Trosley Rd. *Belv* 6E **2**
Trunks All. *Swan* 2A **24**
Truro Rd. *Grav* 3C **22**
Tudor Clo. *Dart* 6G **7**
Tudor Clo. *N'fleet* 1H **21**
Tudor Ct. *Crock* 7B **24**
Tudor Ct. *Sidc* 3D **14**
Tudor Wlk. *Bex* 6H **5**
Tufnail Rd. *Dart* 6A **8**
Tunstock Way. *Belv* 3C **2**
Turnbull Clo. *Grnh* 7F **9**
Turner Ct. *Dart* 5H **7**
Turner Rd. *Bean* 3J **19**
Turners Ct. *W King* 6B **30**
Turners Oak. *New Ash* 3H **31**
Turners Pl. *S Dar* 2D **26**
Turnpike Ct. *Bexh* 4G **5**
Turnstone. *Long* 3D **28**
Turnstones, The. *Grav* 2C **22**
Turpin La. *Eri* 2J **3**
Twigg Clo. *Eri* 7J **3**
Twistleton Ct. *Dart* 6J **7**
Tyeshurst Clo. *SE2* 5C **2**
Tyler Gro. *Dart* 4A **8**
(in two parts)
Tylers Grn. Rd. *Swan* 6B **24**
Tyndall Rd. *Well* 3C **4**
Tynedale Clo. *Dart* 1E **18**
Tyron Way. *Sidc* 4B **14**
Tyrrell Av. *Well* 5D **4**

U

Unicorn Wlk. *Grnh* 5G **9**
University Gdns. *Bex* 7J **5**
University Pl. *Eri* 7G **3**
University Way. *Dart* 4H **7**
(in two parts)
Updale Rd. *Sidc* 4C **14**
Upland Rd. *Bexh* 3J **5**
Up. Abbey Rd. *Belv* 4D **2**
Upper Av. *Ist R* 1H **29**
Up. Church Hill. *Grnh* 5F **9**
Up. Grove Rd. *Belv* 6D **2**
Up. Guild Hall. *Blue* 7G **9**
Up. Holly Hill Rd. *Belv* 5F **3**
Up. Park Rd. *Belv* 4F **3**
Up. Rose Gallery. *Blue* 7H **9**
Upper Ruxley **7K 15**
Up. Sheridan Rd. *Belv* 4E **2**
Upper St. N. New Ash *2J* ***31***
(off Row, The)
Upper St. S. New Ash *2J* ***31***
(off Row, The)
Up. Thames Wlk. *Blue* 1G **19**
Upperton Rd. *Sidc* 5C **14**
Up. Wickham La. *Well* 1E **4**
Upton **5G 5**
Upton Clo. *Bex* 6J **5**
UPTON DAY HOSPITAL 4H **5**
Upton Rd. *Bexh* 4H **5**
Upton Rd. S. *Bex* 6J **5**

46 A-Z Dartford & Gravesend

Upton Vs.—Wood End

Upton Vs. *Bexh* 4H 5
Ursula Lodges. Sidc 5E 14
(off Eynswood Dri.)

V

Valence Rd. *Eri* 7H 3
Valentine Av. *Bex* 2H 15
Vale Rd. *Dart* 1G 17
Vale Rd. *N'fleet* 7G 11
Valley Clo. *Dart* 6E 6
Valley Dri. *Grav* 4C 22
Valley Gdns. *Grnh* 6J 9
Valley Rd. *Belv* 4F 3
Valley Rd. *Dart* 6E 6
Valley Rd. *Eri* 4G 3
Valley Rd. *Fawk* 1D 30
Valley Rd. *Orp* 7E 14
Valley Vw. *Grnh* 6J 9
Valley Vw. Ter. *F'ham* 7A 26
Valliers Wood Rd. *Sidc* 1B 14
Vanessa Clo. *Belv* 5E 2
Vanessa Wlk. *Grav* 5E 22
Vanessa Way. *Bex* 3C 16
Vanquisher Wlk. *Grav* 3E 22
Vaughan Rd. *Well* 2C 4
Vauxhall Clo. *N'fleet* 7J 11
Vauxhall Pl. *Dart* 7K 7
Venners Clo. *Bexh* 2D 6
Venture Clo. *Bex* 7H 5
Veritas Ho. Sidc 2D 14
(off Station Rd.)
Vernon Clo. *W King* 7C 30
Vernon Rd. *Swans* 6C 10
Veroan Rd. *Bexh* 2H 5
Verona Gdns. *Grav* 4D 22
Verona Ho. *Eri* 7K 3
Vestry Cotts. *Long* 4F 29
Viaduct Ter. *S Dar* 2D 26
Via Romana. *Grav* 1G 23
Vicarage Clo. *Eri* 6G 3
Vicarage Ct. *Grav* 1F 23
Vicarage Dri. *N'fleet* 6F 11
Vicarage La. *Grav* 2F 23
Vicarage Rd. *Bex* 1A 16
Vickers Rd. *Eri* 5H 3
Victoria Av. *Grav* 7A 12
Victoria Dri. *S Dar* 2E 26
Victoria Hill Rd. *Swan* 1E 24
Victoria Pk. Ind. Est. *Dart* 5K 7
Victoria Rd. *Bexh* 4K 5
Victoria Rd. *Dart* 5J 7
Victoria Rd. *Eri* 6J 3
(in two parts)
Victoria Rd. *N'fleet* 1J 21
Victoria Rd. *Sidc* 3C 14
Victoria Scott Ct. *Dart* 3E 6
Victoria St. *Belv* 5D 2
Victory Ct. Eri 7K 3
(off Frobisher Rd.)
Victory Way. *Dart* 4D 8
Viewfield Rd. *Bex* 1F 15
View, The. *SE2* 5C 2
Vigilant Way. *Grav* 4D 22
Viking Rd. *N'fleet* 3F 21
Viking Way. *Eri* 3G 3
Viking Way. *W King* 5B 30
Villa Clo. *Grav* 2G 23
Villa Ct. *Dart* 2K 17
Village Cres., The. *Blue* 7G 9
Village Grn. Rd. *Dart* 4F 7
Village, The. *Blue* 7G 9
Vincent Clo. *Sidc* 1B 14
Virginia Wlk. *Grav* 6C 22
Vista, The. *Sidc* 5C 14
Voce Rd. *SE18* 1A 4
Vyne, The. *Bexh* 3A 6

W

Wadard Ter. *Swan* 5H 25
Wadeville Clo. *Belv* 6E 2
Waid Clo. *Dart* 6A 8
Wakefield Rd. *Grnh* 5K 9
Wakefield St. *Grav* 6A 12
Waldeck Rd. *Dart* 7A 8
Walden Clo. *Belv* 5D 2
Waldrist Way. *Eri* 2D 2
Walker Clo. *Dart* 3E 6
Walkley Rd. *Dart* 5G 7
Wallace Clo. *SE28* 1B 2
Wallace Gdns. *Swans* 6B 10
Wallhouse Rd. *Eri* 2K 3
Wallis Clo. *Dart* 3E 16
Wallis Pk. *N'fleet* 5E 10
Walnut Hill Rd. *Grav* 3H 29
Walnut Tree Av. *Dart* 2K 17
Walnut Tree Clo. *Chst* 7A 14
Walnut Tree Rd. *Eri* 5J 3
Walnut Tree Way. *Meop* 6K 29
Walnut Way. *Swan* 2C 24
Walsingham Wlk. *Belv* 6E 2
Waltham Clo. *Dart* 6F 7
Walton Rd. *Sidc* 2F 15
Wansbury Way. *Swan* 5F 25
Wansunt Rd. *Bex* 1B 16
Ward Clo. *Eri* 6H 3
Wardona Ho. *Swans* 6C 10
Wardour Ct. Dart 6C 8
(off Bow Arrow La.)
Waring Rd. *Sidc* 6F 15
Warland Rd. *SE18* 1A 4
Warland Rd. *W King* 7C 30
Warne Pl. *Sidc* 6E 4
Warren Clo. *Bexh* 5K 5
Warren Hastings Ct. Grav 6J 11
(off Pier Rd.)
Warren Rd. *Bexh* 5K 5
Warren Rd. *Dart* 3K 17
Warren Rd. *Sidc* 3F 15
Warren Rd. *S'fleet* 5E 20
Warrens, The. *Hart* 6C 28
Warren, The. *Grav* 4C 22
Warren Vw. *Shorne* 5K 23
Warrior Av. *Grav* 4B 22
Warwick Clo. *Bex* 7J 5
Warwick Ct. *Eri* 7K 3
Warwick Ho. *Swan* 4D 24
Warwick Pl. *N'fleet* 5E 10
Warwick Rd. *Sidc* 5E 14
Warwick Rd. *Well* 3F 5
Warwick Way. *Dart* 2K 17
Watchgate. *Dart* 5E 18
Water Cir. *Blue* 1G 19
Waterdales. *N'fleet* 2F 21
Waterfield Clo. *Belv* 3E 2
Waterhead Clo. *Eri* 7J 3
Water La. *Sidc* 2J 15
(in two parts)
Waterloo St. *Grav* 7B 12
Watermeadow Clo. *Eri* 2K 3
Water Mill Way. *S Dar* 2C 26
Waterside. *Dart* 5D 6
Waterton. *Swan* 4C 24
Waterton Av. *Grav* 7D 12
Watery La. *Sidc* 6E 14
Watling St. *Bean & N'fleet* 2B 20
Watling St. *Bexh* 4A 6
Watling St. *Dart & Bean* 7B 8
Watling St. *Grav & S'fleet* 5A 22
Watson Clo. *Grays* 1H 9
Watts Bri. Rd. *Eri* 6K 3
Wavell Dri. *Sidc* 6B 4
Wayfield Link. *SE9* 6A 4
Waylands. *Swan* 4E 24
Wayville Rd. *Dart* 7C 8
Way Volante. *Grav* 4D 22
Weald Clo. *Ist R* 7H 21
Weardale Av. *Dart* 2D 18
Weavers Clo. *Grav* 1K 21
Weavers Orchard. *S'fleet* 6D 20
Webber Clo. *Eri* 2K 3
Wedgewood Ct. *Bex* 7J 5
Weird Wood. *Long* 3F 29
Weir Rd. *Bex* 7A 6
Welbeck Av. *Sidc* 1D 14
Weldon Way. *Grnh* 5J 9
Wellan Clo. *Sidc* 5E 4
Wellcome Av. *Dart* 4K 7
Well Fld. *Hart* 4C 28
Welling. 3E 4
Welling High St. *Well* 3E 4
Wellington Av. *Sidc* 6D 4
Wellington Pde. *Sidc* 5D 4
Wellington Rd. *Belv* 5D 2
Wellington Rd. *Bex* 5G 5
Wellington Rd. *Dart* 6H 7
Wellington Rd. *Til* 2K 11
Wellington St. *Grav* 7B 12
Welling United F.C. 3F 5
Welling Way. *SE9* 3A 4
Welton Rd. *SE18* 1B 4
Wendover Way. *Well* 5D 4
Wentworth Clo. *Grav* 5K 21
Wentworth Dri. *Dart* 6F 7
Wenvoe Av. *Bexh* 2A 6
Wessex Dri. *Eri* 2D 6
Wessex Wlk. *Bex* 2D 16
Westbourne Rd. *Bexh* 7B 2
Westbrooke Cres. *Well* 3F 5
Westbrooke Rd. *Sidc* 2A 14
Westbrooke Rd. *Well* 3E 4
(in two parts)
Westcott Av. *N'fleet* 3J 21
Westcourt. 2C 22
Westcourt La. *Grav* 1E 22
Westcourt Pde. *Grav* 3D 22
West Cres. Rd. *Grav* 6A 12
Wested La. *Swan* 7F 25
(in two parts)
Westergate Rd. *SE2* 6C 2
Westerham Dri. *Sidc* 6E 4
Western Cross Clo. *Grnh* 6K 9
Westfield. *New Ash* 4J 31
Westfield Clo. *Grav* 6B 22
Westfield Rd. *Bexh* 3B 6
Westgate Rd. *Dart* 6J 7
(in two parts)
Westharold. *Swan* 3C 24
West Heath. 6B 2
W. Heath Clo. *Dart* 6E 6
W. Heath Rd. *SE2* 6A 2
W. Heath Rd. *Dart* 6E 6
West Hill. *Dart* 6J 7
Westhill Clo. *Grav* 1A 22
W. Hill Dri. *Dart* 6H 7
W. Hill Ri. *Dart* 6J 7
West Holme. *Eri* 1B 6
W. Kent Av. *N'fleet* 6F 11
West Kingsdown. 6B 30
W. Kingsdown Ind. Est.
W King 7B 30
West Mill. *Grav* 6J 11
Westmoreland Av. *Well* 3B 4
West Shaw. *Long* 2A 28
West St. *Bexh* 3J 5
West St. *Eri* 4H 3
West St. *Grav* 6K 11
West Ter. *Sidc* 1B 14
W. View Rd. *Crock* 6C 24
W. View Rd. *Dart* 6A 8
W. View Rd. *Swan* 4F 25
Westwood. 7A 20
Westwood La. *Sidc* 5D 4
Westwood La. *Well* 3C 4
Westwood Rd. *S'fleet* 7B 20
West Woodside. *Bex* 1H 15
West Yoke. 3H 31
West Yoke. *Ash* 2G 31
W. Yoke Rd. *New Ash* 3H 31
Wharfedale Rd. *Dart* 1D 18
Wharf Rd. *Grav* 6D 12
Wharfside Clo. *Eri* 5K 3
Wharnecliffe. *Grnh* 6J 9
Wheatley Clo. *Grnh* 5H 9
Wheatley Ter. *Eri* 6K 3
Wheatstone Rd. *Eri* 5H 3
Wheelock Clo. *Eri* 7F 3
Whenman Av. *Bex* 2B 16
Whernside Clo. *SE28* 1A 2
Whinfell Way. *Grav* 4E 22
Whitby Clo. *Grnh* 5H 9
White Av. *N'fleet* 3J 21
Whitecroft. *Swan* 2D 24
Whitegates Av. *W King* 6B 30
Whitehall La. *Eri* 2E 6
Whitehall Pde. *Grav* 3B 22
Whitehead Clo. *Dart* 3H 17
Whitehill La. *Grav* 3B 22
Whitehill Rd. *Dart* 5F 7
Whitehill Rd. *Grav* 2B 22
Whitehill Rd. *Long* 2A 28
White Oak Ct. *Swan* 3D 24
White Oak Gdns. *Sidc* 7C 4
White Oak Sq. Swan 3D 24
(off London Rd.)
White Post Hill. *F'ham* 7B 26
White Post La.
Cobh & Meop 4K 29
Whites Clo. *Grnh* 6K 9
Whitfield Rd. *Bexh* 7D 2
Whitney Wlk. *Sidc* 6H 15
Wickham St. *Well* 2B 4
Wickhams Way. *Hart* 5C 28
Wicksteed Clo. *Bex* 3C 16
Widgeon Rd. *Eri* 2K 3
Wilberforce Way. *Grav* 5C 22
Wilde Clo. *Til* 2B 12
Wilde Rd. *Eri* 7F 3
Wilfred St. *Grav* 6A 12
Wilkinson Clo. *Dart* 4A 8
(in two parts)
Wilks Av. *Dart* 2A 18
Willersley Av. *Sidc* 1C 14
Willersley Clo. *Sidc* 1C 14
William Cory Promenade.
Eri 5J 3
William Ho. *Grav* 7A 12
William Smith Ho. Belv 3E 2
(off Ambrook Rd.)
William St. *Grav* 7A 12
Williams Way. *Bex* 2D 16
Willis Rd. *Eri* 4G 3
Willow Av. *Sidc* 6D 4
Willow Av. *Swan* 3E 24
Willow Clo. *Bex* 6J 5
Willow Grange. *Sidc* 3E 14
Willow Rd. *Dart* 1H 17
Willow Rd. *Eri* 1F 7
Willow Tree Ct. *Sidc* 5D 14
Willow Wlk. *Dart* 5H 7
Willrose Cres. *SE2* 5A 2
Wilmington. 3H 17
Wilmington Ct. Rd. *Dart* 3F 17
Wilmot Rd. *Dart* 5F 7
Wilson La. *S Dar* 2G 27
Wilton Rd. *SE2* 4A 2
Wiltshire Clo. *Dart* 7E 8
Winchelsea Av. *Bexh* 7D 2
Winchester Cres. *Grav* 3C 22
Winchester Rd. *Bexh* 2G 5
Wincrofts Dri. *SE9* 4A 4
Windermere Clo. *Dart* 1G 17
Windermere Rd. *Bexh* 2B 6
Windhover Way. *Grav* 4D 22
Windmill Grange. *W King* 7B 30
Windmill St. *Grav* 6A 12
(in two parts)
Windrush. *SE28* 1A 2
Windsor Dri. *Dart* 6F 7
Windsor Rd. *Bexh* 4H 5
Windsor Rd. *Grav* 3A 22
Wingate Rd. *Sidc* 6F 15
Wingfield Bank. *N'fleet* 2F 21
Wingfield Ct. *Sidc* 2C 14
Wingfield Rd. *Grav* 7A 12
Winifred Rd. *Dart* 5G 7
Winifred Rd. *Eri* 5J 3
Winston Clo. *Grnh* 6G 9
Wintergarden Cres. *Blue* 7H 9
Winters Cft. *Grav* 6C 22
Winton Ct. *Swan* 4D 24
Wise's La. *Stans* 7G 31
Wisley Rd. *Orp* 7D 14
Wisteria Gdns. *Swan* 2C 24
Wodehouse Rd. *Dart* 4B 8
Wolsley Clo. *Dart* 5D 6
Wolvercote Rd. *SE2* 2B 2
Wombwell Gdns. *N'fleet* 2H 21
Wombwell Park. 2G 21
Woodberry Gro. *Bex* 3C 16
Woodbine Rd. *Sidc* 1B 14
Woodchurch Clo. *Sidc* 3A 14
Wood Clo. *Bex* 3D 16
Wood Ct. *Eri* 7J 3
Wood End. *Swan* 4B 24

Woodfall Dri. *Dart* 4D **6**
Woodfield Av. *Grav* 1A **22**
Woodgers Gro. *Swan* 2E **24**
Woodland Av. *Hart* 5C **28**
Woodland Clo. *Long* 3F **29**
Woodlands Av. *Sidc* 1B **14**
Woodlands Clo. *Swan* 3E **24**
Woodlands La. *Shorne* 7J **23**
Woodlands Pk. *Bex* 4C **16**
Woodlands Ri. *Swan* 2E **24**
Woodlands Rd. *Bexh* 3H **5**
Woodlands Ter. *Swan* 6A **24**
Woodland Way. *SE2* 4B **2**
Woodland Way. *Grnh* 5H **9**
Wood La. *Dart* 4E **18**
(in two parts)
Woodlea. *Long* 3F **29**
Woodman Vs. *Fawk* 3E **30**
Woodmount. *Swan* 7C **24**
Woodpecker Rd. *SE28* 1A **2**
Woodside Clo. *Bexh* 4C **6**
Woodside Cres. *Sidc* 3B **14**

Woodside Dri. *Dart* 4D **16**
Woodside La. *Bex* 6G **5**
Woodside Pde. *Sidc* 3B **14**
Woodside Rd. *Bexh* 4C **6**
Woodside Rd. *Sidc* 3B **14**
Woodstock Clo. *Bex* 1J **15**
Wood St. *Swan* 2H **25**
Woodview Clo. *W King* 6B **30**
Woodview Cotts. *Bean* 6H **19**
Woodview Rd. *Swan* 2B **24**
Woodville Gro. *Well* 3D **4**
Woodville Pl. *Grav* 7A **12**
Woodward Ter. *Grnh* 6F **9**
Woolbrook Rd. *Dart* 6D **6**
Woolf Wlk. *Til* 2B **12**
Woollett Clo. *Cray* 4F **7**
Woolwich Rd. *SE2* 6B **2**
Woolwich Rd. *Bexh* 3K **5**
Worcester Clo. *Grnh* 4J **9**
Worcester Clo. *Ist R* 7J **21**
Wordsworth Clo. *Til* 2B **12**
Wordsworth Rd. *Well* 1B **4**

Wordsworth Way. *Dart* 4B **8**
World of Silk. 5D **6**
(off Bourne Rd.)
Wren Rd. *Sidc* 4F **15**
Wrens Cft. *N'fleet* 4H **21**
Wren Wlk. *Til* 1A **12**
Wright Clo. *Swans* 6A **10**
Wrotham Rd. *Ist R & Grav* . . .3J **29**
Wrotham Rd. *Well* 1F **5**
Wyatt Rd. *Dart* 3E **6**
Wycliffe Clo. *Well* 1C **4**
Wycliffe Ho. Grav 1J **21**
(off Wycliffe Row)
Wycliffe Row. *N'fleet* 1J **21**
(in two parts)
Wye Rd. *Grav* 2C **22**
Wyfold Ho. SE2 . . . . .2B **2**
(off Wolvercote Rd.)
Wykeham Clo. *Grav* 6D **22**
Wyncham Av. *Sidc* 1B **14**
Wyncham Ho. Sidc 2D **14**
(off Longlands Rd.)

Wynford Pl. *Belv* 6E **2**
Wyvern Clo. *Dart* 7H **7**

Y

Yarnton Way. *SE2* 2A **2**
Yews, The. *Grav* 2C **22**
Yew Tree Clo. *Long* 2G **29**
Yewtree Clo. *Well* 1D **4**
York Av. *Sidc* 2B **14**
Yorkland Av. *Well* 3C **4**
York Rd. *Dart* 7A **8**
York Rd. *Grav* 3B **22**
York Rd. *N'fleet* 7G **11**
York Ter. *Eri* 1B **6**

Z

Zion Pl. *Grav* 7A **12**

Every possible care has been taken to ensure that the information given in this publication is accurate and whilst the publishers would be grateful to learn of any errors, they regret they cannot accept any responsibility for loss thereby caused.

The representation on the maps of a road, track or footpath is no evidence of the existence of a right of way.

The Grid on this map is the National Grid taken from Ordnance Survey mapping with the permission of the Controller of Her Majesty's Stationery Office.

Copyright of Geographers' A-Z Map Co. Ltd.

No reproduction by any method whatsoever of any part of this publication is permitted without the prior consent of the copyright owners.